beach bach boat barbecue 2

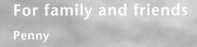

For family and friends

Penny

For my father Peter and my mother Mina, who have always encouraged me to realise my dreams

Ian

First published in 2006 by New
Holland Publishers (NZ) Ltd
Auckland • Sydney • London • Cape Town

www.newhollandpublishers.co.nz

218 Lake Road, Northcote, Auckland,
New Zealand
14 Aquatic Drive, Frenchs Forest,
NSW 2086, Australia
86–88 Edgware Road, London W2
2EA, United Kingdom
80 McKenzie Street, Cape Town 8001,
South Africa

Copyright © 2006 in text: Penny Oliver
Copyright © 2006 in photography: Ian
Batchelor
Copyright © 2006 New Holland Publishers
(NZ) Ltd

ISBN-13: 978 1 86966 110 6

Managing editor: Matt Turner
Design: Christine Hansen
Food stylist: Penny Oliver
Editor: Renée Lang

A catalogue record for this book is available from the
National Library of New Zealand

10 9 8 7 6 5 4 3 2

Colour reproduction by Pica Digital Pte Ltd, Singapore
Printed by Craft Print Pte Ltd

The recipes in this book have been carefully tested
by the author. The publishers and the author
have made every effort to ensure that
the recipes and the instructions
pertaining to them are accurate
and safe but cannot accept liability
for any resulting injury or loss or
damage to property whether direct
or consequential.

beach bach
boat barbecue
2

Food by **Penny Oliver**

Photography by **Ian Batchelor**

NEW HOLLAND

introduction

When Beach Bach Boat Barbecue was published a few years ago, we were thrilled with the way it appeared to strike an immediate chord for so many people throughout New Zealand. We've been thrilled, too, by the fact that its appeal has been ongoing, but the clamour for a sequel could no longer be ignored. And so, here is a brand-new summer collection of easy but stylish casual food, matched with another serving of fellow author Ian Batchelor's luscious food photography and iconic images of the quintessential Kiwi summer.

There is a lot said about how life in the twenty-first century seems to be even more demanding – a far cry from the days when we looked to the future and all that developing technology that promised to give us a better quality of life. So many of us now spend our days dashing from one thing to the other trying to keep up with the demands of family and work life. One thing is certain, though, and that is the importance of a summer holiday to relax and refresh jaded bodies and brain cells. The anticipation starts long before our

tion

annual exodus from the city. Way back in winter we can start to imagine the scent and sound of the sea and entertain thoughts of the long lazy days to come. And then, of course, there are those relaxed meals with family and friends to look forward to – all forming the basis of another set of memories to cherish through the long cold winters to come.

I'd like to point out that as in the first Beach Bach Boat Barbecue, the underlying theme of this book is once again a holiday state of mind. Of course we know not everyone has a bach in the family or access to a boat for that matter. And it really doesn't matter if the dishes within these pages are not literally created at the bach, eaten on the beach or the boat, or enjoyed at a barbecue beside the sea. It's all about context. And as a day at the beach or a barbecue by the lake or river – or for that matter a picnic in your backyard or in the reserve down the road – is within most people's reach, that's the important thing.

We hope you'll enjoy this new four-part serving as much as the first one.

beach

When I was growing up we had a special family and friends ritual in the form of an annual Boxing Day beach picnic. Finding just the right spot with sun, shade and wind protection always used to be the challenge – and the debate was fierce. All the kids would lay out their towels and then a quick directive from the adults ('see who can be the first to get their togs wet!') saw us kids tear off down the beach. Calls of 'swim between the flags!' and 'don't go out too deep!' were distant shouts barely heard, let alone acknowledged by us in the excitement.

Then it was peace at last for the grownups to set up for the day. Bottles of beer and lemonade were strategically placed in the nearest rockpool to cool and after a while it would be time for the picnic

to start. Tasty, but simple, our picnics would always feature a bacon and egg pie, along with staples such as cold saussies and tomato sauce, stuffed savoury eggs, home-grown tomatoes and radishes, and cold meat and chutney sammies. Something sweet would follow, perhaps seasonal stoned fruit or if there were a store nearby we kids would be dispatched to fetch dripping hokey pokey ice creams. The afternoon would be filled with rockpool scavenging, swimming, beach cricket – and a snooze for the grownups. Then it would be time to all pack up the various cars, everyone feeling sunburnt and weary, but reluctantly ready for the drive home. Memories are made of this!

Bread and Roast Tomato Salad

My version of a classic bread salad involves roasting the tomatoes and adding the crunch of pan-toasted almonds.

4 ripe plum or vine-ripened tomatoes, halved
3 cloves garlic, peeled and thinly sliced
sea salt and freshly ground black pepper
pinch of sugar
3–4 tablespoons olive oil
4 thick slices ciabatta bread, torn into pieces
1 red onion, peeled, halved and finely sliced
½ a telegraph cucumber, halved lengthways,
   deseeded and thinly sliced
1 cup blanched pan-toasted almonds
4 tablespoons extra virgin olive oil
2 tablespoons cider vinegar
½ cup finely chopped fresh flat-leaf parsley
1 cup torn fresh basil leaves, loosely packed

Preheat the oven to 180°C. Place the tomatoes cut-side up in a roasting pan and scatter over the garlic, seasonings and sugar. Drizzle over enough olive oil to just moisten each tomato. Roast for 45–60 minutes or until the tomatoes are soft. Fry the bread in the remaining olive oil until crisp and golden. Drain on absorbent kitchen paper and set aside.

To assemble, arrange the tomatoes, onion, cucumber and almonds on a serving platter and drizzle over the extra virgin olive oil and cider vinegar. Allow to stand for 20 minutes at room temperature so the flavours can develop. About 20 minutes before serving, add the bread, parsley and basil and gently fold through the salad. The bread should still be slightly crisp when you serve the salad.

SERVES 4–6

Curried Chicken and Cress Sandwiches

Tuck these moist, mildly spiced chicken sandwiches into your beach picnic or serve for a casual lunch.

1 large cooked chicken, skinned, flesh removed
   and cut into small pieces
½ cup chopped toasted blanched almonds
1¼ cups quality whole egg mayonnaise
½–1 tablespoon good quality curry powder
2 tablespoons sweet tomato chutney
1 teaspoon tomato paste
squeeze of lemon juice to taste
sea salt and freshly ground black pepper
1 loaf sliced brown sandwich bread, each
   slice buttered
fresh watercress or mustard greens

Place the chicken meat, almonds, mayonnaise, curry powder, chutney, tomato paste, lemon juice and seasonings in a bowl and mix together until well combined. Place half the slices of buttered bread on a flat surface and spread each with the chicken filling. Scatter some watercress or mustard greens over the filling. Cover with a buttered slice and gently press down on each sandwich as it is completed. Stack the rounds, wrap in plastic food wrap and refrigerate for 2 hours. Remove 1 hour before serving and cut off the crusts using a very sharp serrated knife or an electric bread knife. Cut into fingers and serve.

MAKES ABOUT 30

Bread and roast tomato salad

Hapuku Fish Cakes

800g firm hapuku fillets
1 clove garlic, peeled and grated
2 fresh red chillies, deseeded and finely
  chopped, or 1 tablespoon Sweet Chilli Salsa (see
  page 14)
sea salt and freshly ground black pepper
grated zest of 1 lemon
vegetable oil for cooking

Chop the fish into pieces, then process in a food processor to form a coarse paste. Transfer to a bowl and add the remaining ingredients. Combine well. Form generous tablespoonfuls of the paste into small fish cakes. Heat 2 tablespoons of oil at a time in a non-stick frying pan over medium heat. Fry the fish cakes in small batches for about 2 minutes on each side until golden. Drain on absorbent kitchen paper and serve with Peanut and Cucumber Salad (see opposite) on the side and lemon or lime 'cheeks'.

SERVES 6

Peanut and Cucumber Salad

Serve alongside fish cakes or vegetable fritters.

1 large telegraph cucumber, peeled, halved
  lengthways, deseeded and diced
2 mild fresh red chillies, deseeded and finely
  chopped
¼ cup fresh coriander leaves
½ cup coarsely chopped raw peanuts,
  pan toasted
3 tablespoons rice wine vinegar
1 tablespoon grated palm sugar or brown sugar
2 tablespoons peanut oil

Place all the ingredients in a bowl and combine. Cover and stand at room temperature for 30 minutes before serving.

SERVES 6

Sweet Chilli Mussels

Sweet chilli salsa lends a spirited kick to mussels. Keep a jar handy in your refrigerator in summer to add to those sauces, marinades and dressings that may need a bit of heat.

SWEET CHILLI SALSA
6 large fresh red chillies, deseeded and chopped
3 cloves garlic, peeled
1 teaspoon grated fresh ginger
1 tablespoon grated palm sugar or brown sugar
¼ cup rice wine vinegar
pinch of salt

¾ cup dry white wine
6 lemon peel curls
½ cup cream
sea salt and freshly ground black pepper to taste
2kg green-lipped mussels, scrubbed and debearded
crusty bread to serve

Place the chillies, garlic and ginger in a food processor and pulse to form a coarse paste. Transfer the paste to a saucepan and add the sugar, vinegar and salt. Simmer gently for 5 minutes until reduced to a syrupy paste.

Place the white wine in a saucepan large enough to hold all the mussels. Add the lemon peel curls, cream, salt and pepper and 4–5 tablespoons of the Sweet Chilli Salsa. Bring to the boil and gently simmer for 5 minutes. Add the mussels to the pan and cover. Simmer for 5 minutes or until the mussels open (discard any that have not opened). Spoon the mussels into serving bowls along with the liquid and serve with chunks of rustic crusty bread. Any remaining salsa will keep in a sealed container in the refrigerator for up to 2 weeks.

SERVES 4

Spiced Squid and Rocket Mayonnaise

500g squid hoods
1 teaspoon sea salt
½ teaspoon cracked black pepper
½ teaspoon lemon pepper
½ teaspoon chilli flakes
vegetable oil for frying

Cut the squid hoods along one side and open them out. Using a sharp paring knife score the inside of each hood in a diagonal pattern, taking care not to cut all the way through. Cut each hood into 8 pieces. Place the seasonings and spices in a small grinder or mini food processor and process until pulverised. Sprinkle the pulverised seasonings over the squid pieces.

Heat the oil in a wok or heavy frying pan over medium–high heat. Fry the squid in batches for 1–2 minutes until it curls and is just cooked through. Drain on absorbent kitchen paper.

Serve immediately with Rocket Mayonnaise (see opposite) for dipping.

Rocket Mayonnaise

Omit the rocket leaves and this recipe will do double duty as a good-quality mayonnaise.

2 egg yolks
1 teaspoon Dijon mustard
1 tablespoon lemon juice
freshly ground black pepper
½ teaspoon sea salt
150ml olive oil
150ml sunflower oil
2 handfuls of rocket leaves

Whisk together the egg yolks, mustard, lemon juice and seasonings. Start adding the oils, a drop at a time, until the mayonnaise thickens. Continue to add the oils in a thin steady stream. If using a blender or food processor, simply drop in the rocket leaves and process them into the mayonnaise. If making the mayonnaise by hand, chop the rocket finely and stir it through.

MAKES ABOUT 1 ½ CUPS

16

Spiced squid and rocket mayonnaise

Pide with Beef and Red Pepper and Pistachio Sauce

PER SANDWICH
pide bread (or focaccia will do)
butter
1 x 2.5cm-thick scotch fillet steak, grilled to taste
salad greens (e.g. iceberg or 'frizzy' lettuce, etc.)
Red Pepper and Pistachio Sauce (see below)
sea salt and freshly ground black pepper

Split the bread and lightly grill the cut sides. Spread butter over the bottom half of each sandwich and arrange a layer of greens over. Cover with a steak and spoon over some Red Pepper and Pistachio Sauce, then sprinkle over seasonings. Cover with the other half of the bread.

Red Pepper and Pistachio Sauce

2 medium red peppers (capsicums)
⅓ cup coarsely chopped pistachio nuts
¼ cup fresh breadcrumbs
2 tablespoons lemon juice
2 tablespoons olive oil
1 teaspoon sambal oelek
½ teaspoon ground cumin
1 teaspoon runny honey
sea salt and freshly ground black pepper to taste

Place the peppers on a hot grill and let the skin blister and blacken slightly on all sides. Set aside to cool. Peel off the skin and slice the flesh, discarding the seeds and membrane.

Place the pepper flesh along with the rest of the ingredients in a food processor and pulse to form a smooth sauce. This sauce will keep in an airtight container for up to 1 week in the fridge.

MAKES ABOUT 1½ CUPS

Prosciutto with Mango and Mint

This fresh light starter, which requires best-quality ingredients, could be assembled on individual plates if you prefer.

2 mangos, skinned, stoned and sliced
12 slices prosciutto
3 tablespoons best-quality extra virgin olive oil
½ cup fresh mint leaves
juice of ½ lemon

Arrange the sliced mangos on a serving platter. Drop the prosciutto slices randomly over the mangos. Drizzle the olive oil over to moisten, then allow the dish to sit at room temperature for 30 minutes. Just before serving, scatter over the mint and squeeze over the lemon juice.

SERVES 4–6

Chicken and Pistachio Meat Loaf

Meat loaves and terrine-style dishes offer versatile summer meal solutions. Serve them hot and moist from the oven, pack them in a picnic, or eat them cold with chutney.

700g minced chicken thigh meat
2 rashers bacon, very finely chopped
2 eggs
½ cup fresh breadcrumbs
1 onion, peeled and finely chopped
½ teaspoon freshly grated nutmeg
½ cup finely chopped flat-leaf parsley
½ teaspoon porcini powder
freshly ground black pepper
8–10 rashers streaky bacon
1 cup pistachio nuts, coarsely chopped

Preheat the oven to 180°C. In a bowl combine the chicken mince, bacon, eggs, breadcrumbs, onion, nutmeg, parsley, porcini powder and pepper until well mixed.

Line a 23cm loaf or terrine dish with the streaky bacon, allowing a generous overhang. Spoon in half the meat mixture, packing it in well. Sprinkle over the pistachio nuts evenly and then spoon in the remaining mixture. Fold the overlapping bacon over the top of the loaf. Cover with aluminium foil to seal. Bake for 1–1¼ hours, removing the foil for the last 5–10 minutes of cooking so that the bacon browns and crisps attractively.

SERVES 6–8

Sweet Tomato Chutney

It's well worth having a few jars of this chutney in your store cupboard over the summer. Best made in small quantities to retain the flavours, it goes well with terrines, barbecued meats, in sandwiches, or served alongside a favourite soft creamy cheese.

1.5kg beefsteak tomatoes, peeled
3 large brown onions, peeled
salt
3 cloves garlic, peeled and crushed
2 red bird's eye chillies, deseeded and chopped
500g brown sugar
1 teaspoon mustard powder
1 tablespoon curry powder
malt vinegar

Cut the tomatoes into quarters and the onions into eighths. Place in a large bowl and sprinkle with salt. Cover and leave overnight. Next day, pour off the liquid and discard. Place the tomato, onion, garlic, chilli, sugar, mustard and curry powder in a large saucepan. Add enough malt vinegar to cover the mixture and bring to the boil. Reduce heat and gently simmer for 1½–2 hours or until thick and pulpy. Pour the chutney into sterilised jars and seal.

MAKES ABOUT 4 SMALL JARS

20

Chicken and pistachio meat loaf with sweet tomato chutney

Meat Loaf

To take this summery meat loaf on a picnic, simply leave it in its loaf tin and cover with fresh aluminium foil. It's more than delicious cut into slices and sandwiched between slices of your favourite bread.

4 slices white bread, crusts removed
100ml milk
1 red onion, peeled and finely diced
1 fresh red chilli, deseeded and chopped
½ cup finely chopped flat-leaf parsley
½ cup torn fresh basil leaves
600g prime ground beef
200g good-quality sausage meat
¼ teaspoon ground nutmeg
2 tablespoons tomato sauce
1 tablespoon Worcestershire sauce
1 egg, beaten
sea salt and freshly ground black pepper to taste
400g cherry or small vine-ripened
   tomatoes, halved
1 teaspoon sugar
1 tablespoon olive oil
fresh basil leaves, extra

Preheat the oven to 200°C. Soak the bread in the milk for 2–3 minutes, then squeeze the bread dry. In a large bowl combine the bread, onion, chilli, herbs, meat, nutmeg, sauces, egg and seasonings. Mix together well. Choose a loaf tin large enough to hold the mixture and pack down firmly. Arrange the halved tomatoes over the top and sprinkle over the sugar and olive oil. Scatter over the fresh basil leaves. Cover with aluminium foil and bake for 45 minutes. Remove the foil and bake for a further 15 minutes.

SERVES 6–8

Bocconcini and Tomato French Toast

Hungry appetites will be well satisfied with this new take on French toast. Better still, everyone can make their own.

PER SANDWICH
1½ tablespoons butter
2 slices fresh white toasting bread
3 slices bocconcini cheese
2–3 fresh basil or chervil leaves
1 small vine-ripened tomato, thickly sliced
1 egg
2–3 tablespoons milk
1 tablespoon olive oil

Use half the butter to lightly spread 1 side of each slice of bread. Place the cheese, basil or chervil and tomato on the buttered side. Cover with the unbuttered slice and firmly press both slices together. In a bowl beat together the egg and milk. Carefully dip the sandwich into the egg mixture, allowing it to soak up all the liquid. Place the remaining butter in a frying pan with the olive oil over medium heat (the pan should be ready as soon as you've dipped the sandwiches). Fry each sandwich for 2–3 minutes on each side until golden and the cheese has melted. Serve immediately.

Roast Olive and Spinach Tart

Delicious served warm in thin wedges alongside barbecued or grilled lamb.

1½ cups plain flour
½ cup grated parmesan cheese
100g chilled butter
pinch of salt
3–4 tablespoons chilled water
1 tablespoon olive oil
1 onion, peeled and finely chopped
2 cloves garlic, peeled and grated
500g fresh spinach leaves, well washed
3 eggs
1 cup crème fraîche
sea salt and freshly ground black pepper
300g roasted olives, pitted and halved
   (available from specialty shops)

Place the flour, cheese, butter and salt in a food processor and pulse until the dough resembles fine breadcrumbs. Add enough of the chilled water so that the dough forms into a smooth ball. Remove from the processor, cover with plastic food wrap and refrigerate for 30 minutes.

Roll out the pastry on a lightly floured board to form a rectangle to fit a 10 x 34cm loose-bottomed tart tin. Cover and refrigerate for a further 30 minutes.

Preheat the oven to 190°C. Heat the olive oil in a frying pan and gently sauté the onion and garlic until soft. Add the spinach and cook until it has just wilted. Drain off any excess liquid and cool mixture. In a bowl beat together the eggs, crème fraîche and seasonings.

Line the chilled pie shell with baking paper and fill with dried beans or uncooked rice to blind bake. Bake for 10–15 minutes. Remove from the oven, allow to cool and remove blind baking materials. Place the cooled shell on a baking tray and spoon in the spinach filling. Pour over the egg mixture and sprinkle over the olives. Return to the oven and bake for 20–25 minutes until the filling is just set.

SERVES 6

Vine-ripened Tomato Salad

This is such a simple, quick tasty salad to serve just about any time, but especially good for a picnic. Seal in an airtight container and enjoy when the time is right.

6 vine-ripened tomatoes, cored
1 red onion, peeled and finely sliced
sea salt and freshly ground black pepper
1 teaspoon brown sugar
2 tablespoons red wine vinegar
2 tablespoons malt vinegar
1–2 tablespoons fish sauce

Cut the tomatoes into wedges and place in a bowl with the onion. Season to taste. Sprinkle over the sugar and gently toss. Drizzle over both kinds of vinegar and the fish sauce and pile into a serving bowl.

SERVES 8–10

25

Smoked Fish and Potato Tart

*Smoky fish, plus creamy eggs spiked with lemon
and dill create a quiche-style tart fit for an
alfresco lunch or brunch gathering.*

**300g good-quality store-bought puff or
flaky pastry**

FILLING
10 egg yolks, beaten
150ml cream
sea salt and freshly ground black pepper
pinch of nutmeg
grated zest of 1 lemon
**500g smoked trevally or snapper, skinned
and flaked**
**2 medium agria potatoes, peeled, cooked
and crushed**
**1 red onion, peeled, halved lengthways and
thinly sliced**
½ cup fresh dill sprigs
lemon 'cheeks'

Roll out the pastry to fit a 30-cm loose-bottomed flan
tin. Fit the pastry into the tin and trim the edges. Prick
the base with a fork and chill for 30 minutes.

Preheat the oven to 200°C. Line the chilled pie shell
with baking paper and fill with dried beans or uncooked
rice to blind bake. Bake for 20 minutes or until the edges
are golden and the base is firm. Remove from the oven,
allow to cool and remove blind baking materials.

While the tart base cools, prepare the filling. Beat
together the yolks, cream, seasonings and lemon zest.
Spread the flaked fish over the cooked and cooled tart
base. Dot with clumps of crushed potato, onion slices
and dill sprigs. Gently pour over the egg mixture and
return the tart to the oven for about 30–35 minutes or
until the filling has just set. Remove from the oven and
serve hot, garnished with lemon 'cheeks'.

SERVES 8

Chicken Dogs

*A quick, tasty and easy light meal that will be
popular with all ages.*

4 skinless boneless chicken breasts
½ cup Barbecue Basting Sauce (see page 113)
8 hot dog rolls, halved lengthways
olive oil
16 buttercrunch lettuce leaves

Cut the chicken breast into strips and then into chunks.
Place the chopped chicken in the sauce and marinate
for 2 hours.

Remove the chicken from the marinade and grill on a
barbecue plate, over medium heat, basting the chicken
with the sauce as it cooks. Brush the cut side of the rolls
with a little oil and grill on the barbecue until lightly
charred. When the chicken is cooked, place 2 lettuce
leaves on each roll, add some chicken and top with the
other half of the roll. Wrap each roll in a paper napkin
and serve.

MAKES 8

Smoked fish and potato tart

Picnic Pies

*Serve for a special brunch or wrap them in
aluminium foil and tuck into the picnic basket.*

olive oil
12 bread slices, crusts removed
12 thin slices prosciutto
12 free-range eggs
12 vine-ripened cherry tomatoes
1 tablespoon chopped chives
2 tablespoons cheese, grated or crumbled
  (parmesan, pecorino, or feta)
sea salt and freshly ground black pepper

Preheat the oven to 180°C. Lightly oil a 12-cup muffin
pan. Line the bottom of each cup with a bread slice and
arrange a slice of prosciutto to encircle. Break an egg
into each bread case. Top with a tomato and sprinkle
with a few chives, a little cheese and seasonings. Bake
for 15–20 minutes or until the egg is set and beginning
to shrink from the sides. Remove the pan from the oven
and run a knife around the sides of each cup to loosen
the pies and remove.

MAKES 12

Iceberg Wedges with Dijon Avocado Sauce

*You can't beat the crunch of iceberg lettuce. Pep
it up with this creamy avocado sauce that you
could also use as a dipping sauce if you were to
serve this salad on an outdoor picnic.*

1 large firm iceberg lettuce, heart core removed
1 ripe avocado, peeled and stoned
1 teaspoon Dijon mustard
2 tablespoons lemon juice
2 teaspoons Sweet Chilli Salsa (see page 14)
sea salt and freshly ground black pepper
¼ cup olive oil

Cut the lettuce into sixths and arrange on a serving
platter.
   Place the avocado flesh, mustard, lemon juice, Sweet
Chilli Salsa and seasonings in a food processor. With the
motor running, slowly drizzle in the olive oil until the
dressing is thick and creamy. Spoon the dressing over
the lettuce and serve immediately.

SERVES 6

Sweet Barbecue Ribs

Prepare these ribs in the morning ready for the evening barbecue. The sticky sweet bones will be enjoyed by children and grown-ups alike.

3 small pork racks, cut into single ribs
1 tablespoon olive oil
4 cloves garlic, peeled and crushed
½ cup tomato purée
½ cup pineapple juice
½ cup balsamic vinegar
¼ cup soy sauce
½ cup honey
sea salt and freshly ground black pepper

Place the ribs in a shallow pan. Combine the remaining ingredients and pour over the ribs to coat. Transfer the pan to the fridge and marinate for 2 hours.

Remove the ribs from the marinade, brushing off any excess. Retain the marinade.

Barbecue the ribs over medium heat for 20–30 minutes or until well browned, cooked and caramelised on the outside. Place the remaining marinade in a saucepan and reduce by half over low heat. When the ribs are done place on a serving plate and pour over the reduced marinade. Serve immediately.

SERVES 6

Sweet barbecue ribs

Roasted Salmon, Cucumber and Pickled Walnut Sandwiches

Rich salmon flavours are cut with the sharp acidity of apple cider vinegar, pickled walnut and fresh mint to produce a smart sandwich to serve with evening drinks when friends gather.

1 loaf sliced white sandwich bread
softened butter for spreading
crème fraîche
1 telegraph cucumber, peeled and thinly sliced
apple cider vinegar
8 pickled walnuts, thinly sliced
400g hot roasted salmon
freshly ground black pepper
handful of fresh mint leaves

Butter each slice of bread right to the very edge. Spread each slice with a thin layer of crème fraîche. Place the cucumber in a shallow dish. Pour over enough apple cider vinegar to moisten and set aside for 5 minutes. Drain the cucumber on absorbent kitchen paper, then place a layer of it over half of the bread slices. Top the cucumber with slices of pickled walnut, then a thin layer of salmon. Season to taste then add some mint. Cover with a buttered slice and gently press down on each sandwich. Stack the rounds, wrap in plastic food wrap and refrigerate for 1 hour. When ready to serve, remove the crusts using a very sharp serrated knife or an electric bread knife. Cut into quarters and arrange on a plate.

MAKES ABOUT 40

Chocolate Louise slice

Chocolate Louise Slice

Perfect to serve with coffee or pack to take on a picnic.

80g butter
4 tablespoons caster sugar
3 eggs, separated
1½ cups plain flour
1 teaspoon baking powder
1 tablespoon cocoa
½ cup caster sugar, extra
1 cup shredded coconut
½ cup raspberry jam
2 cups fresh or frozen raspberries

Preheat the oven to 180°C. Cream the butter and sugar until light and pale. Add the egg yolks, one at a time. Gradually fold in the sifted flour and baking powder and cocoa to form a dough. Line a 21 x 25cm baking tin with a sheet of baking paper to fit. Press the dough evenly over the base of the tin, then chill while you prepare the topping.

Beat the egg whites until they form soft peaks, then gradually add the extra caster sugar and continue to beat until the meringue is thick and shiny. Fold in the coconut.

Spread the raspberry jam over the chilled base, then add a layer of raspberries. Gently spread the meringue on top. Bake for 40 minutes. Remove from the oven and run a knife around the edge to loosen the slice. Cool in the pan before cutting into slices.

MAKES 20–24 PIECES

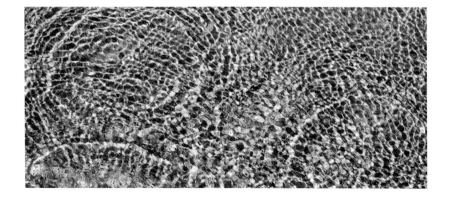

Apricot and Ricotta Pastry Slice

200g fresh ricotta cheese
⅓ cup chopped dark chocolate
½ cup mixed peel
grated zest of 1 lemon
⅔ cup icing sugar
1 tablespoon brandy or cognac
2 apricots, halved, stoned and finely chopped (or use tinned apricots)
370g puff pastry
milk for brushing
¼ cup flaked almonds
icing sugar for dusting
whipped cream, mascarpone or Yoghurt Cheese Balls (see page 40)
   to serve

Place the ricotta, chocolate, peel, lemon zest, icing sugar and brandy in a food processor and pulse to combine. Stir in the chopped apricots and refrigerate until ready to use. Roll out the pastry on a lightly floured board to form a 20 x 30cm rectangle, then transfer to a baking tin lined with baking paper. Chill for 20 minutes.

Preheat the oven to 180°C. Spread the chilled ricotta and apricot mixture down the middle third of the pastry. Fold over both sides to enclose the filling and press down the length of the join with your fingers to seal. Brush with a little milk and sprinkle over the flaked almonds.

Bake for 20–25 minutes or until the pastry is puffed and golden. Turn onto a wire rack to cool. Dredge with a little icing sugar and serve warm with whipped cream, mascarpone or Yoghurt Cheese Balls.

SERVES 6

Apricot and ricotta pastry slice

bach

Coastal developments in recent years have made quite a big difference to the meaning of the word 'bach'. For most people who grew up in the second half of the twentieth century, a bach used to be a single man's dwelling, hence the name (from 'bachelor'). They could be found up and down the country and coastline, most featuring much-patched corrugated iron roofs and paint-blistered and peeling exterior wooden walls. Inside there'd be a hotchpotch of cast-off furniture and old crockery. Over time these shacks or baches became holiday homes for so many Kiwis (but if you were of Celtic stock and particularly if you lived in the southern South Island, you would know them as cribs, a word that used to mean a building to house livestock).

In all its dilapidated glory, the bach or crib became the family summer retreat from everyday life, whether this was in the city or out in the rural back-blocks. It was a place where over the years family traditions evolved, good times were had by family and friends, and cherished memories began to build up. Today the word 'bach' remains in our language, but its modern metamorphosis has seen it change from a place with just one room for sleeping and another for eating and living to luxurious waterside homes worth millions of dollars crammed with every conceivable aid to modern living. The essence of retreating to the bach remains, however. It will always be a place where you go to get away, to enjoy the outdoors with family and friends, to relax with a good book, and especially to enjoy a bottle of luscious wine and some simple, tasty bach cuisine.

Salmon Tempura and Palm Sugar Dipping Sauce

Serve this delicate battered salmon as an individual starter or as pre-dinner finger food.

2 eggs
150ml sparkling mineral water, chilled
salt
¾ cup plain flour
⅓ cup cornflour
1 tablespoon grated lime zest
1 tablespoon lime juice
500g fresh skinless salmon fillet cut into 1cm strips
sunflower oil for frying
lime 'cheeks' to serve

Break the eggs into a bowl with the mineral water and whisk gently to combine. Add the salt, flours, lime zest and lime juice and combine with a fork. The batter should be a little lumpy. Heat enough oil to deep-fry the fish – ideally in a wok or a heavy-bottomed frying pan. The oil should be hot enough (190–200°C) so that when a piece of bread is dropped in, it turns golden in 30 seconds. Dip the salmon strips in the batter and fry in batches for 2–3 minutes. Drain on paper towels and arrange on a platter with lime 'cheeks' alongside some Palm Sugar Dipping Sauce (see below) in a small bowl.

SERVES 4

Palm Sugar Dipping Sauce

2 tablespoons grated palm sugar
2 tablespoons rice vinegar
2 tablespoons lime or lemon juice
2 tablespoons olive oil
1 teaspoon wasabi
1 medium fresh red chilli

Whisk the first 5 ingredients together. Garnish with a few slices of fresh chilli.

Yoghurt Cheese Balls

Versatile yoghurt cheese (or labna) can be used to make these savoury bites, or serve alongside a dessert as a healthy substitute for cream or mascarpone.

500g plain acidophilus yoghurt
nuts or seeds to coat (e.g. sumac, sesame seeds, freshly chopped herbs, chopped toasted pine nuts, zatar)

Rinse a 20 x 20cm square of muslin under cold water and squeeze dry. Line a sieve with the muslin and set over a bowl. Spoon in the yoghurt, then place in the refrigerator to drain for 1–2 days. The longer the draining time, the firmer the cheese will be. The yoghurt cheese will keep for up to 10 days in an airtight container in the refrigerator.

Roll the thick yoghurt cheese into small bite-sized balls, then roll in the coating of choice. Chill for 1 hour before serving whole or spread on some flatbread and serve with an evening 'sundowner'.

MAKES ABOUT 20 LITTLE BALLS

Salmon tempura and palm sugar dipping sauce

Artichoke and Cannellini Dip

1 cup marinated artichoke hearts, drained
1 x 400g can cannellini beans, drained
1 clove garlic, peeled and crushed
¼ cup finely grated parmesan cheese
3 teaspoons lemon juice
3 tablespoons flat-leaf parsley
freshly ground black pepper and sea salt to taste
½ cup olive oil

Place the drained artichoke hearts, beans, garlic, parmesan, lemon juice, parsley and seasonings in a food processor and pulse together to break up the ingredients. With the motor running, drizzle in the olive oil to form a thick paste. Serve with Grilled Flat Bread (see opposite).

MAKES 2 CUPS

Grilled Flat Bread

450g strong white bread flour
7g dried yeast
1 teaspoon salt
300ml tepid water

Place the flour, yeast and salt in a large bowl. Make a well in the centre and pour in the tepid water. Mix to form a soft, non-sticky dough. Turn out onto a lightly floured board and knead the dough vigorously for 5 minutes or until smooth. Return to the bowl and cover with plastic food wrap and leave in a warm place until doubled in size. Knock down the dough with your fist and turn onto a floured board. Divide the dough into about 16 pieces. Roll each piece into a smooth ball, then flatten to form individual rounds about 13cm in length.

Heat a large frying pan until hot (or heat a barbecue grill plate). Cook the bread rounds for about 1 minute on each side or until just cooked through.

MAKES ABOUT 16 PIECES

Rice Paper Rolls

Typical Asian flavours and textures mingle with a crunch inside these baby wraps.

1 cup finely shredded Chinese cabbage
½ cup coarsely grated carrot
¼ cup chopped mint leaves
¼ cup chopped coriander leaves
2 tablespoons chopped chives
1 tablespoon shredded pickled ginger
2 tablespoons raw peanuts, pan-roasted and
   coarsely chopped
12 x 16cm rice paper rounds
12 tiger prawns, cooked, shelled and deveined

SAUCE
4 tablespoons rice wine vinegar
2 tablespoons sweet chilli sauce
1 teaspoon lemon juice

In a large bowl combine the cabbage, carrot, mint, coriander, chives, pickled ginger and peanuts. Place the rice paper rounds, one at a time, in a bowl of warm water until they soften slightly. Lift carefully from the water, place on absorbent kitchen paper and dry each side. Transfer to a board and place one-twelfth of the cabbage mixture in the centre of the round. Top with a prawn. Fold in the sides and roll up. Repeat the process with the remaining rice paper rounds.

Combine the ingredients for the sauce and serve alongside the rolls.

MAKES 12 ROLLS

Pan-fried Mushrooms and Chicken Livers on Toast

A truly delicious start to a meal for all those lovers of chicken livers.

80g butter
1 small red onion, peeled and sliced
50g mushrooms, sliced
¼ cup chopped fresh sage leaves
¼ cup chopped flat-leaf parsley
200g chicken livers, trimmed and chopped
   in quarters
¼ cup cabernet merlot
sea salt and freshly ground black pepper
1 clove garlic, peeled
8 slices rustic country-style bread, toasted
fresh sage leaves for garnishing

Heat the butter in a frying pan over low to medium heat. Add the onion and cook until soft. Add the mushrooms, herbs and chicken livers and increase the heat to medium. Cook the livers for 4–5 minutes or until they are still slightly pink in the middle. Turn up the heat to high and add the wine and seasonings. Cook for 1 minute, then remove from the heat. Cut the garlic clove in half and rub over the toasted bread, then brush with a little olive oil. Spoon the mushrooms and livers onto the toasted bread and garnish with fresh sage leaves.

SERVES 4 AS A STARTER

Rice paper rolls

Couscous and Cheese Patties

1½ cups cooked couscous
150g haloumi cheese
120g sheep's feta cheese
grated zest of 1 lemon
freshly ground black pepper
¾ cup flat-leaf parsley
vegetable oil for cooking

Place the couscous, both kinds of cheese, lemon zest, pepper and parsley in a food processor and pulse until the mixture resembles breadcrumbs. Shape into 10–12 patties and place on a plate. Cover with plastic food wrap and chill for 30 minutes.

Heat enough vegetable oil in the bottom of a heavy-bottomed or non-stick frying pan to just cover the base. Fry the cakes in batches for 2–3 minutes on each side until golden. Serve with a crisp salad and a little Tomato and Chilli Jam (see page 97).

SERVES 4–6

Summer Salad

A pert salad with clean fresh summer flavours and a smooth rich dressing.

2 vine-ripened tomatoes, blanched, skinned
    and deseeded
1 firm ripe avocado, halved, stoned, skinned
    and chopped
1 fennel bulb, finely sliced
1 shallot, peeled and finely sliced
1 lemon, peeled, pith removed and flesh diced
¼ cup black olives, pitted
2 cups baby spinach leaves, washed, dried
    and fridge-crisp

DRESSING
1 teaspoon Dijon mustard
½ cup olive oil
1 tablespoon fresh orange juice
1 tablespoon sherry vinegar
sea salt and freshly ground black pepper

Arrange all the salad ingredients on a serving platter. To make the dressing, whisk the olive oil slowly into the mustard so it forms an emulsion. Flavour the emulsion with the orange juice, vinegar and seasonings to taste, adjusting if necessary. Drizzle the dressing over the salad and serve.

SERVES 6

Couscous and cheese patties with summer salad

Green Salad

1 cup broad bean kernels, blanched, cooled
and dried
handful of french beans, blanched and halved,
cooled and dried
1 cup fresh peas, blanched, cooled and dried
handful of snow peas, thinly sliced
handful of snow pea shoots
1 cup finely chopped flat-leaf parsley
1 cup chopped chives
sea salt and freshly ground black pepper
peppery extra virgin olive oil
lemon juice

Combine all the vegetables and herbs on a serving plate
and gently toss together. Just before serving, season to
taste and drizzle over a little olive oil and lemon juice to
moisten.

SERVES 6–8

Potato and Pecorino Rosti with Egg and Salmon

*For perfect poached eggs, have the poaching
water just shimmering with a dash of vinegar and
salt.*

1kg waxy potatoes, unpeeled
½ cup grated pecorino cheese
freshly ground black pepper
2 tablespoons vegetable oil
50g butter
6 eggs, poached
300g smoked salmon
fresh crisp cos lettuce leaves

Place the potatoes in a saucepan of cold water. Bring to
the boil and simmer for 10 minutes. Drain and cool. Peel
the potatoes and then coarsely grate them into a bowl.
Stir in the pecorino and season to taste with the pepper.
Allow to cool completely. Place half the oil and half the
butter in a medium heavy-bottomed frying pan over
medium heat. When the oil and butter bubbles, add the
potato mixture and gently press down and outwards
with an egg slice to cover the pan. Turn down the heat
to low and cook for 10 minutes or until bottom is golden
and crisp. Invert onto a plate. Add the remaining oil and
butter to the pan. Slide the rosti back into the pan and
cook the other side for 10 minutes or until crisp. Divide
into six wedges and top each with a poached egg, some
smoked salmon and several cos lettuce leaves.

SERVES 6

Salmon and Beetroot Salad with Horseradish Dressing

Enriched with hot and roasted salmon, this pretty and elegant salad lends itself to a lady-like summer lunch.

1 raw beetroot, peeled and coarsely grated
   (about 1 cup)
1½ cups rocket leaves
1½ cups watercress leaves or equivalent amount
   of other fresh greens
200g fresh ricotta cheese
400g hot roasted salmon, broken up
200g feta cheese, crumbled
1 small bulb fennel, sliced very finely
1 small red onion, peeled and sliced finely

HORSERADISH DRESSING
2 tablespoons hot horseradish sauce
3 tablespoons thick yoghurt
1 tablespoon sherry vinegar
2 tablespoons lemon juice
4 tablespoons extra virgin olive oil
sea salt and freshly ground black pepper
pinch of caster sugar

Drain the raw beetroot on absorbent kitchen paper. Arrange the greens over a serving platter. Scatter the raw beetroot among the greens. Dot with the remaining salad ingredients.

Combine the dressing ingredients and drizzle over the salad. Serve immediately.

SERVES 6

Spiced Carrots

6–8 medium carrots, peeled and cut into
   chip-sized chunks
2 cloves garlic, peeled and grated
4 tablespoons good-quality peppery extra virgin
   olive oil, plus a little extra if required
1–2 tablespoons zatar
2 tablespoons red wine vinegar
sea salt and freshly ground black pepper
pinch of brown sugar

Blanch and drain the carrots. Dry with absorbent kitchen paper. Gently fry the garlic in the olive oil over medium heat for about 2 minutes. Add the carrots, zatar, vinegar, seasonings and brown sugar. Toss the carrots in the pan until they are coated with the seasonings and just warmed through. Add a little extra olive oil to moisten them if required.

SERVES 6

Salmon and beetroot salad with horseradish dressing

Crispy Pan-fried Snapper with Almond Tarator Sauce

The secret to successful crispy skin is to have the cooking pan or barbecue plate at the right heat.

6 x 130g snapper fillets, skin on
plain flour for dusting
ground sea salt
olive oil for cooking

TARATOR SAUCE
1 clove garlic, peeled and grated
sea salt
½ cup whole blanched almonds, toasted
½ cup fresh white breadcrumbs
2 tablespoons lemon juice
¾ cup olive oil
2 tablespoons boiling water

Dust the snapper with flour and season with salt. Heat the oil on a barbecue plate or in a frying pan over high heat. Fry the snapper skin-side down for approximately 4 minutes or until crisp. Turn over and cook the other side for 1–2 minutes.

To make the sauce, place the garlic, salt, almonds and breadcrumbs in a food processor and pulse until finely chopped. Add the lemon juice. With the motor running, add the olive oil in a thin steady stream until emulsified. Transfer to a bowl and then stir in the water to form a smooth thick sauce. Serve the sauce alongside the crisp snapper.

SERVES 6

Citrus and Fennel Salad

The light refreshing citrus and aniseed flavours in this delicious salad will complement grilled and pan-fried white fish and salmon.

2 pomelo
3 ruby grapefruit
2 oranges
1 lime
1 fennel bulb, finely sliced
1 shallot, finely chopped
young fennel leaves
olive oil
sea salt to taste

Peel all the citrus fruit, then separate into segments, retaining all the juice. Place the segmented fruit, fennel and shallot and the fennel leaves on a serving plate. Mix together the citrus juice and olive oil to taste. Drizzle over enough of this dressing to moisten the salad and season to taste.

SERVES 6–8

Crispy pan-fried snapper with almond tarator sauce
and citrus and fennel salad

Spiced Roasted Pork Loin

Ask your butcher to score the skin before the meat is rolled.

2kg rolled pork loin
1 tablespoon fennel seeds, crushed
1 teaspoon ground cumin
1 tablespoon honey, redcurrant jelly or
   brown sugar
¼ cup apple cider vinegar
sea salt

Score the rind of the pork closely across the top ensuring the cuts go through the flesh. Combine the fennel seeds, cumin and honey, jelly or sugar and massage into the scored skin. Drizzle over the cider vinegar and marinate in the fridge for 2 hours.

Preheat the oven to 200°C. Rub a generous amount of sea salt into and over the scored skin. Place the pork in a roasting pan and cook for 30 minutes, then reduce the heat to 160°C for 1 hour or until the juices run clear when tested. If the skin is not crispy enough raise the temperature and cook for a further 5–10 minutes. Alternatively, place the pork under a hot grill until the skin blisters and crisps. Stand pork for 15 minutes before carving and serve with Apple Salsa Verde (see opposite).

SERVES 6–8

Apple Salsa Verde

4 sweet apples (such as Gala), peeled, cored
   and diced
2 tablespoons water
2 tablespoons apple cider vinegar
¼ cup caster sugar
1½ cups flat-leaf parsley
10 fresh basil leaves
10 fresh mint leaves
1 tablespoon Dijon mustard
1 tablespoon drained capers
150ml olive oil
sea salt and freshly ground black pepper

Place the apple, water, vinegar and sugar in a saucepan and simmer with the lid on for 10 minutes or until the apples are just tender. Place the herbs, mustard, capers and oil in a food processor or blender and pulse to a purée. Season to taste. Transfer to a bowl and fold through the apple. Cover and allow to stand for 30 minutes before serving with Spiced Roasted Pork Loin.

Roast Chicken Salad

This flavoursome bold salad makes a great dish for a buffet-style meal if you are entertaining a crowd.

12 chicken portions, skin on, bone in

MARINADE
2 cloves garlic, peeled and finely chopped
⅓ cup verjuice
¼ cup extra virgin olive oil
1 bay leaf

olive oil
½ cup chicken stock
2 tablespoons verjuice

SALAD
3 tablespoons extra virgin olive oil
2 rashers streaky bacon, thinly sliced
3 slices ciabatta bread, torn into bite-sized pieces
½ cup fresh walnuts, chopped
½ cup cherry tomatoes, halved
1 cup seedless green grapes, halved
1½ cups rocket leaves
finely sliced rind of ½ preserved lemon, flesh discarded
sea salt and freshly ground black pepper to taste
1½–2 tablespoons red wine vinegar
2 tablespoons coarsely chopped flat-leaf parsley

Place the chicken in a plastic container that can be firmly sealed. Combine the marinade ingredients and pour over the chicken. Cover and refrigerate for 2 hours, turning occasionally.

Preheat the oven to 180°C. Remove the chicken from the marinade and dry on absorbent kitchen paper. Heat some olive oil in a large frying pan over medium–high heat and brown the chicken pieces in batches. Transfer to a roasting pan and bake for 15 minutes or until the chicken is cooked. Remove from the oven and pour the stock and verjuice over. Return to the oven but turn off the heat.

To make the salad, heat the oil in a frying pan over medium heat and brown the bacon and bread pieces until crisp. Add the walnuts, cherry tomatoes and grapes to the pan and cook for 1 minute. Remove the warm chicken from the oven and transfer, along with the juices, to a serving platter. Add the rocket leaves, preserved lemon, seasonings and vinegar to the pan and toss to combine. Spoon over the chicken, then sprinkle over the parsley.

SERVES 6

Roast chicken salad

Buttermilk Scones with Berry Jam and Mascarpone

375g (1½ cups) self-raising flour
1 tablespoon icing sugar or caster sugar
pinch of salt
40g soft butter
1¼ cups buttermilk, plus extra for brushing
Berry Jam (see opposite)
250g mascarpone
icing sugar

Preheat the oven to 220°C. Sift together the flour, sugar and salt. Using your fingertips, rub in the butter until the mixture resembles fine breadcrumbs. Make a well in the middle and pour in the buttermilk. Stir with a fork to form a soft dough. Turn out on a floured board and lightly knead (about 10–12 times) until the dough forms a ball. Roll out to form a 2cm-thick rectangular shape. Using a 5.5cm cutter, cut out rounds and place on a baking tray lined with baking paper. Brush the tops with buttermilk. Bake for 15 minutes or until golden and risen. Cool on a wire rack.

To serve, halve the scones and fill with Berry Jam and mascarpone. Dredge the tops with icing sugar.

MAKES 12 LARGE OR 16 SMALL SCONES

Berry Jam

Making this type of jam is so simple – utilise summer berries when they are at their cheapest and most plentiful so that you can have summer at your fingertips all year round. Berry Jam is perfect for queen puddings, trifles, tarts, Louise cake or on grainy toast, croissants and the classical Devonshire tea.

1kg white sugar
1kg strawberries, or raspberries, boysenberries or mixture
75ml lemon juice
50g jam setter (available at supermarkets)

Preheat the oven to 180°C. Place the sugar in an ovenproof bowl and warm for 5 minutes in the oven. Wash and hull the berries, then place with the lemon juice in a saucepan over low heat. Gently cook for 20 minutes, stirring until the berries are soft. Add the warm sugar and jam setter and cook for a further 5 minutes or until the sugar dissolves. Increase the heat to medium until the jam comes to a gentle rolling boil. Cook for a further 5 minutes. Test a teaspoonful of the jam on a cold saucer. If it wrinkles when you run your finger through the sample it's ready; if not cook further and re-test. Allow the jam to sit for 10 minutes off the heat before ladling into sterilised jars and sealing.

MAKES ABOUT 4 SMALL JARS

Summer Pudding

½ cup caster sugar
¼ cup water
¼ cup cassis (blackcurrant liqueur)
2 cups strawberries, hulled and halved
3 cups fresh raspberries
2 teaspoons lemon juice
150ml cream
2 tablespoons icing sugar
1 teaspoon vanilla extract
250g mascarpone
about 20 Italian sponge finger biscuits
fresh strawberries and raspberries for garnishing

Combine the caster sugar, water and cassis in a saucepan and simmer until the sugar dissolves. Add the strawberries and cook for 2 minutes. Remove from the heat and stir through the raspberries. Add the lemon juice and stir to combine. Strain the fruit from the syrup and set aside, retaining syrup. In a bowl whip together the cream, icing sugar and vanilla until thick. Fold the mascarpone through this mixture and set aside.

Dip half the sponge fingers one at a time in the syrup, then use them to line the bottom of a small lasagne dish or equivalent. Evenly spoon the lightly cooked berries over the sponge fingers. Add a layer of mascarpone and spread it out evenly. Dip the remaining sponge fingers in the cassis syrup and layer them over the top – do not discard the syrup. Tightly cover the pudding with plastic food wrap, then weigh the top down with some plates and refrigerate overnight. Spoon the pudding straight from the dish or loosen the edges with a knife dipped in hot water for 20 seconds and then invert onto a serving dish and serve in slices. Strain the remaining syrup of crumbs and drizzle a little over the pudding along with some extra berries for garnish.

SERVES 8–10

Summer pudding

Chocolate Raspberry Cake

A classic combination of chocolate and almond combined with tart seasonal raspberries makes this cake a rich delectable dessert.

100g dark chocolate, coarsely chopped
1 cup cream
125g butter
1¼ cups firmly packed brown sugar
3 eggs
1 cup self-raising flour
¼ cup Dutch cocoa
½ cup ground almonds
⅓ cup raspberry jam
⅓ cup raspberries, mashed

GLAZE
200g dark chocolate, melted
⅔ cup thickened cream

Combine the chocolate and cream in a bowl and microwave on low heat until it melts. Stir together to combine, then set aside to cool.

Preheat the oven to 150°C. Grease a 22cm loose-bottomed cake tin. In a separate bowl cream the butter and brown sugar until pale. Beat in the eggs, one at a time. Stir in the cool chocolate and cream mixture. Sift in the flour and cocoa and fold through the mixture. Mix in the ground almonds. Spread the mixture in the prepared cake tin and bake for 1¼ hours. Allow the cake to cool in the tin for 15 minutes before removing to a wire rack to cool.

Split the cake horizontally through the middle and spread the jam and scatter the raspberries over one half. Top with the other half of the cake. Melt together the chocolate and thickened cream and stir until smooth. Allow the mixture to cool and as it begins to thicken spread it over the top and sides of the cake.

SERVES 8–10

Pavlova with Pomegranate

No traditional New Zealand meal would be complete without a version of this fluffy melt-in-the-mouth dessert.

4 egg whites
1 cup caster sugar
1 tablespoon cornflour
1 teaspoon malt vinegar
300ml cream
1 teaspoon pure vanilla extract
1 tablespoon icing sugar
1 pomegranate

Preheat the oven to 140°C. Grease and line an oven tray with baking paper. Draw an 18–20cm circle on the baking paper.

In a bowl beat the egg whites with a beater until they form soft peaks. Gradually add the sugar, a little at a time, beating constantly until the mixture is stiff and shiny. Fold in the cornflour and vinegar. Spread the meringue inside the circle on the tray and level the top with a spatula. Bake for 1¼ hours or until the meringue is firm. Turn off the oven and leave the pavlova to cool in the oven with the door ajar.

Beat together the cream, vanilla and icing sugar until it forms soft peaks. Spread the cream over the cooled meringue. Cut the pomegranate in half and scoop out the seeds and juice (discard shell). Spoon the seeds and juice over the cream.

SERVES 6–8

Roly Poly Pudding

1⅓ cups plain flour
1 tablespoon baking powder
115g unsalted butter, chopped into small pieces
¼ cup caster sugar
150ml water
2 tablespoons raspberry jam
2 cups fresh mixed summer berries
2 tablespoons milk
1 tablespoon demerara sugar

Preheat the oven to 160°C. Sift the flour and baking powder into a bowl and stir in the chopped butter. Using your fingertips, rub the butter into the flour until the mixture resembles fine breadcrumbs. Stir in the caster sugar. Slowly add the water, stirring, until the mixture combines. Roll out the dough on a lightly floured board to form a 24 x 36cm rectangle. Spread the jam over the surface leaving a 2cm border. Evenly sprinkle over the berries. Roll up along the long edge. Place the rolled-up dough seam-side down in a baking-paper-lined lamington tin or a low-sided baking pan. Brush with the milk and sprinkle over the demerara sugar. Bake for 30–40 minutes or until golden and cooked through. Serve with ice cream.

SERVES 6–8

Pavlova with pomegranate

Christmas Bombe

An excellent, chilled, light citrus replacement for a traditional steamed Christmas pudding.

non-stick cooking spray oil
75g mixed peel
⅓ cup limoncello liqueur
500g mascarpone
100g caster sugar
300ml thickened cream
2 x Crunchie bars, coarsely chopped

Spray a 1.5 litre pudding basin with the oil and line with plastic food wrap. Place the mixed peel and limoncello in a saucepan and simmer over low heat for 5 minutes, then cool. Beat together the mascarpone and caster sugar until smooth, then add the thickened cream, mixed peel in limoncello and chopped Crunchie bars. Fold together and spoon into the prepared pudding basin. Cover and freeze overnight.

To serve, transfer the bombe to the refrigerator for 20–30 minutes so it softens a little. Turn out onto a cold serving platter. Slice into wedges and serve with fresh seasonal sliced stone fruit or berries.

SERVES 6

boat

An evening sail, a putter in the dinghy or a full-on summer cruise ... a meal out of a chilly bin, a six-course banquet prepared in a sophisticated galley or a barbecue on the back of the boat or riverbank. Whatever your circumstances, the common denominator here is water and how wonderfully relaxed it makes us feel when we're near it – whether it's by the sea or perhaps a lake or even a favourite swimming spot at the local river.

To spend a day fishing, diving and swimming, waterskiing or doing nothing at all other than simply enjoying the ambience of lapping waters and isolated beaches away from it all, what better therapy for the jaded soul? Given the hectic pace of daily life, the lure of an escape to more natural surroundings is stronger than ever. For me, boating holidays are all about being so relaxed that the time of day becomes irrelevant. Sleeping, reading, swimming and eating fill the day, but not in any particular order.

If someone catches a fish or two, well, that's dinner. And how sensational fresh fish tastes straight from the sea. A few minutes to gut and scale it and then it's straight onto the hot grill. A squeeze of fresh lemon juice, a grind of black pepper and mmmmm – perfection.

Scallops with Tarragon Pesto

Scallops look sensational served in the shell — and these ones are so easily cooked on the barbecue, whether on the boat, beach or at the bach.

36 scallops, cleaned, each placed in a half shell

TARRAGON PESTO
½ cup tightly packed tarragon leaves, stripped from the stem
1 clove garlic, peeled and grated
¼ cup pan-toasted pine nuts
¼ cup freshly grated parmesan cheese
1–2 tablespoons lemon juice plus extra for drizzling
grated lemon zest
5 tablespoons olive oil plus extra for drizzling

Keep the scallops chilled until ready to cook. Place the tarragon leaves, garlic, pine nuts, parmesan, lemon juice and lemon zest in a food processor and pulse to combine. While the motor is running, drizzle in olive oil. Remove to a bowl or container of choice and set aside until ready to use.

Place 1 teaspoon of pesto in each scallop shell and drizzle with just a little of the extra olive oil. Place the shells on a preheated barbecue or under a grill for 2–3 minutes to cook the scallops. Remove to a serving plate and finish with a squeeze of lemon juice.

SERVES 6

Scallops with tarragon pesto

Salted Almonds

A handy nibble to have in your store cupboard.

1 egg white
200g unblanched almonds
¼ cup flaked sea salt

Preheat the oven to 200°C. Whisk the egg white to form stiff peaks. Add the almonds and stir the nuts through until they are well coated. Line a baking tray with baking paper and spread the almonds evenly over the tray in a single layer. Sprinkle with the salt and bake for 15 minutes or until the egg white and salt are crusty. Remove from the oven and cool. Store in an airtight jar.

Spinach, Avocado and Egg Salad

Vary this delicious lunchtime salad with the addition of a little sliced red onion, or sliced sun-dried tomato if you prefer, and serve with some warm country-style bread.

300g baby spinach leaves (about 3 good
handfuls), washed and dried
6 rashers bacon, prosciutto, speck or pancetta,
grilled crisp
3 slices bread, torn into bite-sized pieces and
fried in a little olive oil until golden and crisp
olive oil for cooking
1 avocado, halved, stoned, peeled and sliced
3 soft-boiled eggs, shelled and halved
¼ cup flaked parmesan cheese

DRESSING
1 clove garlic, peeled and grated
sea salt and freshly ground black pepper
2 tablespoons red wine vinegar
4 tablespoons extra virgin olive oil

Place the spinach leaves in a plastic bag and refrigerate for 1 hour until really crisp.

Arrange the spinach on a platter and add the remaining ingredients so they form layers among and on top of the crisp leaves. Combine the dressing ingredients and drizzle over the salad just before serving.

SERVES 6

Zatar Soldiers

6 slices moist, dense grainy bread
½ cup zatar
4 tablespoons extra virgin olive oil
2 tablespoons lemon juice
sea salt to taste
1 small firm ripe avocado, halved, stoned,
    peeled and diced
¼ cup chopped chives

Toast the bread until golden. Mix the zatar, olive oil, lemon juice and salt together to form a thick paste. Taste to check the flavours and add a little extra olive oil or lemon juice if necessary. Spread the paste evenly over the toast right to the edge of each piece. Cut into 'soldiers' and top with the diced avocado and chopped chives.

MAKES ABOUT 18

Marinated Olives

Experiment with the strength of the flavours if you like. Marinated olives are a great store-cupboard ingredient to have at hand to add to salads or to serve as a quick nibble.

800g black olives in brine
2 tablespoons fennel seeds, crushed
1 tablespoon green cardamom pods, crushed
1 tablespoon flaked chilli
finely sliced rind of ¾ preserved lemon, flesh
    discarded
9 fresh bay leaves
¼ cup runny honey
1 cup olive oil
extra olive oil to cover

Rinse the olives in cold water, drain and dry on absorbent kitchen paper. Place the spices in a frying pan and toast over moderate heat for a few minutes until they pop and become aromatic. Remove from the heat and place in a bowl along with the lemon, bay leaves and honey. Stir together with 1 cup of olive oil. Add the olives and mix to coat with the aromatic oily mixture. Spoon into 3 x 500ml sterilised jars, ensuring each one has about the same amount of bay leaves, spices and lemon peel. Top up the jars with olive oil to just cover the olives. Seal and leave for at least 1 week before serving. The flavour improves with age and will keep for 3–4 months.

MAKES 3 JARS

Zatar soldiers

Grilled Ham, Cheese and Spinach Tortilla Sandwiches

You can easily produce these tasty sandwiches using bought tortillas from the galley or off the barbecue plate.

1 packet soft flour tortillas (packets usually contain 8)
2 teaspoons Dijon mustard
400g grated gruyère cheese
3 good handfuls of baby spinach leaves
400g thinly sliced leg ham

Place half the tortillas on a flat surface and spread each with ½ teaspoon of mustard. Add a layer of evenly spread grated cheese, spinach leaves and ham, then top with a plain tortilla. Carefully place the sandwiches one at a time on a heated sandwich grill or in a frying pan and press it down gently but firmly. Cook for 3–4 minutes or until golden on the bottom, then turn to cook the other side until the cheese is melted and the spinach wilted. Remove to a flat surface and cut each sandwich into quarters. Serve immediately.

MAKES 16 SANDWICHES

Couscous Salad

Make this salad well ahead of time to allow the flavours to develop.

450g instant couscous
1 cup finely chopped flat-leaf parsley
½ cup finely chopped fresh mint leaves
2 tomatoes
2 cloves garlic, peeled and grated
¼ cup lemon juice
¼ cup extra virgin olive oil
sea salt and freshly ground black pepper

Prepare the couscous according to the packet instructions, then transfer to a bowl. Add the remaining ingredients and mix together, adjusting the quantity of lemon juice, olive oil and seasonings to your taste.

SERVES 6

Grilled ham, cheese and spinach tortilla sandwiches

Baked Side of Salmon

Serve cold with mayonnaise (see page 16) or Chilli Mango and Pineapple Salsa (see opposite) as part of a buffet-style meal or on bruschetta with drinks.

½ cup light soy sauce
2cm piece fresh ginger, peeled and finely grated
2 cloves garlic, peeled and grated
4 tablespoons honey
2 tablespoons Sweet Chilli Salsa (see page 14)
1.5kg side fresh salmon, skin on
olive oil
juice of 1 lime
sea salt and freshly ground black pepper

Mix together the first 5 ingredients. Pour into a shallow dish just large enough to contain the salmon fillet. Place the salmon into the marinade, flesh-side down. Cover and marinate in the fridge for 1 hour.

Preheat the oven to 200°C. Remove the salmon from the marinade. Tear off a generous piece of aluminium foil large enough to contain the salmon, and fold up around the edges. Brush the foil with olive oil and place the salmon on it, skin-side down. Squeeze over the lime juice and season to taste. Fold over the edges of the foil so that the salmon is entirely enclosed. Fold in the ends to seal. Place the foil package in a roasting pan and bake for 15 minutes. Remove from the oven and leave in the foil to cool. When ready to serve, unroll the foil and remove the skin. Serve the fish marinated-side up.

SERVES 6

Chilli Mango and Pineapple Salsa

Delicious with baked, grilled or roasted salmon.

½ fresh pineapple, skinned, cored and
  finely diced
1 fresh red chilli, deseeded and finely chopped
1 mango, skinned and flesh finely diced
1 small red onion, peeled and finely chopped
¼ cup chopped mint
¼ cup chopped flat-leaf parsley
2 tablespoons lemon or lime juice

In a bowl combine all the ingredients. Cover and allow to stand for 30 minutes at room temperature so the flavours can develop.

MAKES ABOUT 2 CUPS

Crayfish Cocktail

A simple but classic way to give everyone a taste of this sweet delicate flesh.

1 cooked crayfish, about 2kg
2 tablespoons finely chopped chives
chopped rind of ¼ preserved lemon, flesh discarded
¼ cup finely chopped flat-leaf parsley
sea salt and freshly ground black pepper
grated zest of 1 lime
2 tablespoons lime juice
1 large firm ripe avocado, stoned, peeled and chopped
½ iceberg lettuce, finely shredded

DRESSING
½ cup Mayonnaise (see page 16)
1 tablespoon tomato sauce
1 teaspoon Tabasco sauce
1 tablespoon lemon juice
lime 'cheeks' for garnishing

Pull the crayfish tail away from the body in one piece and halve the tail lengthways. Lift out the meat and discard the intestinal tract. Slice the flesh into bite-sized pieces. Place the crayfish, chives, preserved lemon, parsley, salt and pepper, lime zest, lime juice, avocado and shredded lettuce in a bowl and gently toss together. Spoon into 6 serving glasses. Combine the mayonnaise with the rest of the dressing ingredients. Spoon a little over the top of each cocktail and garnish with lime 'cheeks'.

SERVES 6

Crayfish cocktail

Corn Cob Fritters

3 fresh corn cobs, husks and silk removed
¼ cup chopped chives
¼ cup chopped flat-leaf parsley
sea salt and freshly ground black pepper
½ teaspoon dried chilli flakes
¾ cup plain flour
1 teaspoon baking powder
3 eggs
olive oil for cooking

Using a sharp knife remove the kernels from the cobs. Place two-thirds of the kernels in a food processor along with the herbs, seasonings, chilli flakes, flour, baking powder and eggs. Pulse to form a batter. Transfer the batter to a bowl and stir in the remaining corn kernels.

Place enough olive oil to just cover the bottom of a frying pan over medium heat. Allowing about 2 tablespoons of batter per fritter, drop ladlefuls of the mixture into the hot frying pan, 2 or 3 at a time. Cook fritters until golden brown on one side, then turn to cook the other side.

MAKES 8 SUBSTANTIAL FRITTERS

Avocado Mash

2 vine-ripened tomatoes, skinned, deseeded and
  coarsely chopped
1 avocado, halved, stoned and peeled
2 spring onions, thinly sliced
1 small red chilli, deseeded and finely chopped
2 tablespoons chopped fresh coriander
2 tablespoons lemon juice
sea salt and freshly ground black pepper to taste

Drain the tomatoes on absorbent kitchen paper for about 10–15 minutes. Chop avocado flesh, then place in a bowl. Fold in all the other ingredients and serve alongside Corn Cob Fritters (see opposite).

Corn cob fritters and avocado mash

Bacon and Onion Tart

Tasty tarts are particularly convenient to take for a day out in the boat.

400g flaky pastry
200g fresh ricotta cheese
¾ cup grated parmesan cheese
¼ cup chopped flat-leaf parsley
2 brown onions, peeled and thinly sliced
2 cloves garlic, peeled and grated
¼ cup olive oil
pinch of sugar
4 slices streaky bacon, finely sliced
2 cups cherry tomatoes
sea salt and freshly ground black pepper

Roll out the pastry on a lightly floured board to fit a 30cm loose-bottomed tart tin. Refrigerate the pastry while you prepare the filling. Combine the ricotta, parmesan and parsley in a bowl and set aside. Preheat the oven to 160°C.

In a heavy-bottomed frying pan cook the onion and garlic in the olive oil with a pinch of sugar over medium heat until soft and golden. Spread the cheese mixture over the chilled pastry. Spoon over the cooked onion mixture, then top with the streaky bacon, cherry tomatoes and seasonings. Bake for 45–50 minutes or until the pastry is puffed and golden.

SERVES 6–8

Bacon and onion tart

Crisp Barbecued Pork Belly

Try these pork belly strips served with either Chilli Mango and Pineapple Salsa (see page 79), or Tangelo and Pine Nut Relish (see opposite).

2 cloves garlic, peeled and grated
1 tablespoon grated fresh ginger
¼ cup runny honey
¼ cup orange marmalade
¼ cup sweet Thai chilli sauce
½ cup pineapple juice
4 tablespoons lime or lemon juice
3 tablespoons kecap manis
2kg pork belly strips, each 2.5cm thick,
  rind removed

Combine the first 8 ingredients in a small saucepan and gently simmer over low heat until the sauce begins to reduce and thicken. Allow the sauce to cool, then pour it over the pork strips. Cover and marinate in the fridge overnight, ensuring the meat is well coated in the marinade.

Drain the pork, reserving the marinade. Grill the pork on a preheated grill plate, brushing occasionally with the reserved marinade until each rib is cooked through and is golden and crisp.

SERVES 4–6

Tangelo and Pine Nut Relish

Spice up grilled chicken, pork and fish with a spoonful of this remarkably delicious and quick-to-make fresh relish.

1½ cups segmented tangelo pieces,
  juice reserved
½ cup pan-toasted pine nuts, coarsely chopped
1 teaspoon grated fresh ginger
1 tablespoon lemon juice
1 tablespoon pomegranate molasses
1 tablespoon olive oil

Chop the tangelo segments in half. Place all the ingredients, including any juice, in a bowl and fold together.

MAKES ABOUT 2 CUPS

Linguine with Prawns, Chilli and Summer Herbs

Quick and easy to cook, pasta is a convenient ingredient to store on board the boat. Vary the seafood depending on availability. Scallops are a good substitute.

500g linguine
¾ cup extra virgin olive oil
3 cloves garlic, peeled and grated
400g cooked cleaned prawns
pinch of dried chilli flakes
1 long fresh red chilli, deseeded and finely chopped
2 large vine-ripened tomatoes, skinned, deseeded and chopped
¼ cup chopped flat-leaf parsley
¼ cup chopped mint leaves
¼ cup chopped rocket leaves
2 tablespoons lemon juice
grated zest of 1 lemon
sea salt and freshly ground black pepper

Cook the linguine in a large saucepan of salted water until al dente, then drain and set aside.

Meanwhile heat half the olive oil in a frying pan over medium heat. Add the garlic, prawns and both kinds of chilli. Cook, stirring, for 1 minute or until the prawns are heated through. Stir in the chopped tomato. Add the parsley, mint, rocket, lemon juice and zest and toss together. Add the drained linguine, remaining olive oil and season to taste.

SERVES 4

Linguine with prawns, chilli and summer herbs

Parmesan Crumbed Fish Fillets

1½ cups breadcrumbs made from day-old bread
½ cup grated parmesan cheese
grated zest of 1 lemon
6 white fish fillets (e.g. snapper, tarakihi,
    or hapuku)
plain flour seasoned with sea salt and freshly
    ground black pepper
2–3 eggs, beaten with 1 tablespoon milk
olive oil for cooking

Combine the breadcrumbs, parmesan and lemon zest
and mix together. Using tongs, dust the fish fillets with
the seasoned flour, shaking off any excess. Dip into the
beaten egg and then coat in the breadcrumb mixture.
Place the crumbed fish on a flat platter lined with baking
paper and refrigerate for 1 hour prior to cooking.

Heat enough olive oil to just cover the bottom of a
frying pan over medium heat. Fry the fish in batches
for 2 minutes on each side or until golden, then drain
on absorbent kitchen paper. Serve with a crisp salad or
barbecued seasonal vegetables and a little Tangelo and
Pine Nut Relish (see page 86).

SERVES 6

91

Lemon Roasted Chicken and Potatoes with Green Olives

olive oil
1.5kg small gourmet potatoes (e.g. jersey bennes)
2 red onions, peeled and cut into eighths
4 cloves garlic, peeled and sliced
2 bay leaves
2 corn-fed chickens, jointed with skin left on
freshly ground black pepper
sliced rind of 1 preserved lemon, flesh discarded
½ cup chicken stock
1½ cups green olives (e.g. Picholine olives)

Preheat the oven to 180°C. Drizzle enough olive oil in the bottom of one large or two smaller roasting pans to just cover. Spread the potatoes, onion, garlic and bay leaves over the bottom in a single layer. Arrange the chicken pieces on top and season with the pepper. Tuck in the preserved lemon rind around the chicken. Pour over the chicken stock and scatter over the olives. Roast for 45 minutes to 1 hour or until the chicken is golden and cooked through. Arrange on a serving platter and serve with Spiced Carrots (see page 50).

SERVES 6–8

Lemon roasted chicken and potatoes with green olives

Barbecued Fish with Lemon and Herb-infused Olive Oil

A divine and simple way to cook that freshly caught fish.

2–3 lemons
225ml best-quality extra virgin olive oil
2 cloves garlic, peeled and grated
¼ cup coarsely chopped flat-leaf parsley
sea salt and freshly ground black pepper
6 x 350g whole snapper, cleaned and scaled
extra freshly squeezed lemon juice, olive oil and seasonings

Grate the zest from the lemons and squeeze the juice into a bowl. Add the olive oil, garlic, parsley and seasonings to taste and mix together. Cover and allow to stand for 1 hour.

Wash and dry the fish inside and out. Using a sharp knife, cut several slashes into the sides of each fish. Season the outside of the fish with the extra lemon juice, olive oil, sea salt and pepper and massage it into the fish. Heat the flat plate on the barbecue to medium–high heat. Place the fish on the plate and cook for 4–5 minutes on each side or until cooked through. Place the cooked fish on a serving plate and pour over the dressing.

SERVES 6

Tomato and Chilli Jam

This punchy store-cupboard jam can transform the ordinary into extra-tasty. Serve alongside grilled and barbecued meat and poultry, simple meat loaves, terrines or egg dishes.

1kg ripe beefsteak tomatoes, chopped
1 cup sugar
¼ cup vegetable oil
4 shallots, peeled and finely chopped
4 cloves garlic, peeled and grated
6 long fresh red chillies, sliced (leave seeds in)
1 teaspoon prawn paste
100g palm sugar, grated
100g fish sauce
100ml tamarind water
2cm piece fresh ginger, grated

Place the tomatoes and sugar in a bowl. Cover and leave overnight at room temperature. Next day heat the oil in a heavy-bottomed saucepan over medium heat and fry the shallots and garlic until soft. Add the chillies and prawn paste and cook gently for 10 minutes. Stir in the palm sugar, fish sauce, tamarind water and ginger and cook for 2–3 minutes. Add the tomato mixture and reduce the heat. Simmer for 1 hour or until thick. Pour into sterilised jars and seal.

MAKES 3 CUPS

Coconut Lime Log

125g butter, softened
2 teaspoons grated lime zest
1 cup caster sugar
4 eggs
2 cups ground almonds
1 cup self-raising flour, sifted
1 tablespoon lime juice
¼ cup lime juice, extra
¾ cup caster sugar, extra
¼ cup shredded coconut, toasted

Preheat the oven to 160°C. Beat the butter, lime zest and sugar together until light and fluffy. Add the eggs, one at a time, beating well after each addition. Stir in the ground almonds, flour and first measure of lime juice. Spoon into a 20 x 10cm greased loaf tin or 12 x ½-cup capacity greased non-stick muffin pans. Bake for 45–50 minutes (if in a tin or 20–25 minutes in muffin pans) until an inserted skewer comes out clean. Combine the second measure of lime juice and caster sugar and spoon a little over each cake while still warm in the pans. Sprinkle the top with the coconut just before serving warm with whipped cream or yoghurt cheese.

SERVES 8–10

Chocolate Nut Biscotti

These keep well – and eat well with a morning coffee or enjoy them dunked into your favourite after-dinner liqueur tipple.

1 cup raw nuts, pan-roasted and coarsely
   chopped (e.g. almonds, hazelnuts, brazil nuts,
   pine nuts, macadamia nuts)
1⅔ cups plain flour
2 tablespoons Dutch cocoa
½ teaspoon baking powder
½ teaspoon cinnamon
¾ cup caster sugar
3 eggs, beaten
grated zest of 1 orange

Preheat the oven to 200°C. Place the prepared nuts in a bowl. Sift in the flour, cocoa, baking powder and cinnamon. Stir in the sugar. In a separate bowl combine the eggs and orange zest and gradually add to the dry ingredients, stirring to form a dough. Turn the dough onto a lightly floured surface. Lightly knead the dough to bind together, then divide in half. Shape each piece into a 25cm log. Place on a baking tray lined with baking paper. Bake for 15 minutes, then remove from the oven and allow to stand for 10 minutes. Slice the logs into 5mm thick slices and lay them flat on the baking tray. Bake for a further 10 minutes or until dryish. Cool on a wire rack. Store in an airtight container.

MAKES 40

Coconut lime log

Passionfruit and Lemon Olive Oil Cake

5 eggs
⅔ cup caster sugar
grated zest of 1 lemon
50ml light olive oil
1 tablespoon passionfruit pulp
1 cup plain flour, sifted
2 tablespoons icing sugar
whipped cream or mascarpone to serve

LEMON AND PASSIONFRUIT SAUCE
¼ cup lemon juice
2 tablespoons caster sugar
3 fresh passionfruit, halved and pulp reserved

Preheat the oven to 160°C. Grease a 23cm springform cake tin and line it with baking paper. Using an electric beater, whip the eggs, sugar and lemon zest together until the mixture triples and is thick and pale. Continue to beat, adding the olive oil drop by drop to start with and then in a thin, slow steady stream. Stir in the first quantity of passionfruit pulp. Sift the flour again into the mixture, then gently fold it in with a metal spoon. Pour into prepared cake tin and bake for 25–30 minutes or until springy and shrinking away from the sides of the tin. Cool for 10 minutes in the tin, then turn onto a wire rack. Dust the top with icing sugar.

For the sauce, combine the ingredients in a small saucepan over medium heat. Serve the cake with a dollop of whipped cream or mascarpone, and a drizzle of lemon and passionfruit sauce.

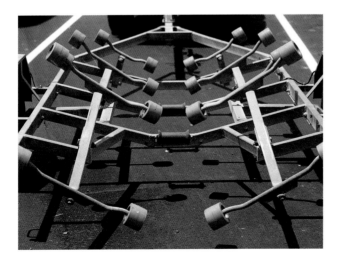

Passionfruit and lemon olive oil cake

Walnut and Coffee Cakes

It's so easy to pack these sweet soft morsels into an airtight container. They will remain moist for 3 days. You can dress them up, too – simply drizzle them with a little extra espresso coffee and a dollop of mascarpone.

150g fresh walnuts, finely ground
1⅔ cups self-raising flour
250g caster sugar
100g unsalted butter, softened
2 eggs
½ teaspoon vanilla extract
100ml freshly brewed espresso, cooled

COFFEE ICING
2 cups icing sugar, sifted
1 tablespoon instant coffee powder
1 teaspoon melted butter
1–2 tablespoons lemon juice
12 fresh walnut halves

Preheat the oven to 160°C. In a bowl combine the ground walnuts and flour. In a separate bowl cream together the sugar and butter until light and fluffy. Beat in the eggs one at a time. Stir in the vanilla, then the flour and walnut mixture alternately with the coffee until just combined. Spoon the mixture into ½-cup capacity greased muffin pans. Bake for 20–25 minutes or until an inserted skewer comes out clean. Remove the cakes from the pans while hot and transfer to a wire cooling rack.

To make the icing, place the icing sugar, coffee and butter in a bowl and combine. Drip in enough lemon juice to stir the icing to a thick smooth paste. When the cakes are cool, smear them generously with icing and top each with a walnut half.

MAKES 12

boat

Fig and Strawberry Caramel Tarts

Make these at home before you embark on an evening cruise and dinner on board with friends. Serve with some marinated fresh strawberries on the side.

2 sheets pre-rolled sweet shortcrust pastry
1 can caramelised condensed milk
12 strawberries, halved
2 fresh figs, each cut into 6 wedges

Using an 8cm biscuit cutter, cut 6 rounds from each sheet of pastry. Grease a 12 x ½-cup capacity muffin pan and carefully line each cavity with a round of pastry. Chill for 20 minutes.

Preheat the oven to 160°C. Cut out 12 squares of baking paper to fit the pastry-lined cavities in the muffin pans. Place the baking paper squares in each pastry round and fill with uncooked rice to weigh them down. Blind-bake the tarts for 15 minutes or until they begin to brown and firm up. Remove from the oven and take out the rice and paper. Carefully remove the tart shells to a wire rack to cool. To assemble the tarts, spoon in the caramelised condensed milk and top each tart with two strawberry halves and a wedge of fresh fig.

MAKES 12

Fig and strawberry caramel tarts

barbecue

The concept of the Kiwi barbecue has changed as outdoor living becomes more sophisticated. Other than on the beach, it's extremely rare these days to find those old cut-down tin drums over an outdoor fire – a style of cooking that not only showed Kiwi ingenuity at its best, but formed the basis of many special holiday memories.

Competition for the most glamorous kind of outdoor cooking is now fierce – lidded kettle-style barbies on tripods, sophisticated stainless steel gas-guzzlers or full-on purpose-built outdoor barbecue kitchens – they all compete to satisfy our primordial urge to cook with fire. Even the hard-nosed 'can't cook/won't cook' members of the family find it hard to resist the lure of the flames that are part of this sensual form of socialising.

But whether it's burned bangers with tomato sauce (affectionately known by many Kiwis as 'train smash') or any of the recipes offered in this chapter, the undisputed fact about barbecuing is that food cooked outdoors over a flame of some kind always tastes better.

Cheese, Tomato and Herb Bruschetta

Experiment with other toppings on your choice of cheese, for example, tapenade, sun-dried tomatoes or herb pesto.

1 stick sourdough bread cut into 16 x 1cm slices
2 cloves garlic, peeled and halved
500g cheese (e.g. mozzarella, bocconcini, creamy
    blue, goat's cheese or feta)
4 tomatoes, skinned, deseeded, drained
    and chopped
selection of chopped fresh herbs to complement
    the cheese (e.g. basil, chopped chives,
    flat-leaf parsley, rocket, oregano)
extra virgin olive oil

Lightly grill or toast the bread on both sides until lightly charred. Rub one side of each slice with the cut garlic. Top with a layer of cheese, then tomato and chopped herbs. Drizzle with a little oil to moisten the topping.

MAKES 16

Eggplant, Mint and Ricotta Salad with Lemon and Cumin Dressing

2 medium eggplants (aubergines), cut into
    1cm-thick slices
8 tablespoons olive oil
sea salt and freshly ground black pepper
100g fresh ricotta cheese
1 cup small mint leaves

LEMON AND CUMIN DRESSING
⅓ cup extra virgin olive oil
1 small clove garlic, peeled and grated
1 tablespoon lemon juice
1 tablespoon runny honey
½ teaspoon ground cumin

Brush the eggplant slices on both sides with olive oil. Grill over a medium–hot barbecue until lightly charred and tender. Arrange on a serving platter and season. Dot with the ricotta and sprinkle over the mint leaves. Combine all the dressing ingredients and whisk together. Drizzle the dressing over the eggplant. Serve with barbecued lamb or chicken.

SERVES 6

Cheese, tomato and herb bruschetta

Broad Bean, Lime and Coriander Dip

2 cups broad bean kernels
1 tablespoon chopped preserved lemon rind,
  flesh discarded
1 clove garlic, peeled and finely chopped
1 teaspoon ground cumin
½–¾ cup olive oil
2 tablespoons lemon or lime juice
sea salt and freshly ground black pepper to taste
¼ cup chopped fresh coriander

Place the broad bean kernels, lemon rind, garlic, cumin, oil and lemon juice in a food processor and blend until it forms a thick paste. Season to taste. Thin with a little more lemon juice if too thick. Cover and refrigerate to develop the flavours.

Just before serving, stir in the fresh coriander and accompany with fresh crisp raw vegetables or flat bread.

MAKES 2 CUPS

Barbecued Corn with Garlic and Chilli Butter

6 fresh corn cobs
4 tablespoons butter
2 cloves garlic, peeled and coarsely grated
1 fresh red chilli, deseeded and chopped
¼ cup chopped flat-leaf parsley

Remove the husks and silk from the corn. Cook the cobs in salted boiling water for 5 minutes, then drain. Melt the butter in a frying pan on the barbecue. Add the garlic and chilli and gently cook over low heat for 5 minutes to infuse the flavours. Grill the cobs on a medium hot grill for 5 minutes until lightly charred, brushing with some of the melted butter as they cook. Transfer the cooked cobs to a serving platter. Stir the parsley through the remaining butter and spoon over the corn.

SERVES 6

Broad bean, lime and coriander dip

Barbecue Basting Sauce

Keep a supply of this basting sauce when barbecuing is at its peak. It's wonderful over sausages, steaks, hamburgers and cheaper cuts of meat.

200ml tomato passata
50ml tomato sauce
50ml white wine vinegar
50ml maple syrup
2 tablespoons Worcestershire sauce
1 tablespoon Dijon mustard
2 cloves garlic, peeled and grated
½ teaspoon smoked paprika

Place all the ingredients in a small saucepan and simmer gently for 10 minutes until the sauce has reduced and thickened slightly. Cool and store in an airtight container in the fridge for up to 10 days.

MAKES ABOUT 1 CUP

Char-grilled Skewered New Potatoes

1kg medium new potatoes, washed and unpeeled
4 tablespoons olive oil
sea salt and freshly ground black pepper
bamboo skewers, pre-soaked in cold water
    for 1 hour

Cook the potatoes in boiling salted water until just tender, about 15 minutes. Drain the potatoes and allow to cool. Cut the potatoes in half and toss gently in a bowl with the olive oil and seasonings. Thread the potatoes onto the skewers and grill on a medium heat until heated and lightly charred.

SERVES 4

Barbecued Tomatoes

500g vine-ripened tomatoes, halved
6 cloves garlic, peeled and finely chopped
1 tablespoon chopped oregano leaves
1 teaspoon brown sugar
¼ cup olive oil
sea salt and freshly ground black pepper
bamboo skewers, pre-soaked in cold water
    for 1 hour

Place the first 6 ingredients in a bowl and marinate for 1 hour. Drain the tomatoes, reserving the oil for basting, then thread them evenly onto the skewers. Place on a medium to hot barbecue plate and grill for 5–7 minutes or until lightly charred and slightly softened. Turn and baste with the reserved oil during cooking.

SERVES 4–6

Barbecued Mushrooms with Bocconcini

12 rashers streaky bacon
12 medium Portobello mushrooms, wiped clean
   and stalks trimmed
extra virgin olive oil
3 bocconcini, each sliced into 4 rounds
12 sun-dried tomatoes, halved
12 basil leaves
lemon juice
freshly ground black pepper

Cook the bacon until crisp. While the bacon is cooking, place the mushrooms on a medium–hot barbecue plate and drizzle each with 1 teaspoon of oil. Cook, stalk-side down, for 2–3 minutes, then turn mushrooms and place 2 slices of bocconcini on each. When the cheese melts, top each mushroom with a sun-dried tomato, a crisp bacon rasher and some fresh basil. Squeeze over a slurp of fresh lemon juice and some black pepper. Serve immediately.

SERVES 6

Barbecued mushrooms with bocconcini

Barbecued Stuffed Fillet of Beef with Walnut Salsa

1kg centre-cut piece eye fillet
1 shallot, peeled and finely chopped
2 cloves garlic, peeled and grated
2 tablespoons olive oil
1 cup fresh walnuts, coarsely chopped
1 cup marinated artichoke hearts, coarsely
    chopped
200g baby spinach leaves
sea salt and freshly ground black pepper

Trim the fillet of all sinew and fat. Butterfly the fillet (slice down the centre two-thirds of the way through, then open it out on both sides like a book). Use a rolling pin to roll and pound it to achieve an even 1cm thickness. Sauté the shallot and garlic in the olive oil over low heat until soft. Stir in the walnuts, artichoke hearts, spinach and seasonings. Cook briefly until the spinach wilts. Remove from the heat and allow to cool.

Spread the filling over the butterflied meat. Roll up on the long side as tightly as possible, tying at 2cm intervals along the length. Sear the meat on a barbecue plate over high heat until golden on all sides. Reduce the heat to medium, cover and grill for 15 minutes. Remove from the heat and allow to rest for 15 minutes before carving. Serve sliced with Walnut Salsa (see opposite).

SERVES 6

Walnut Salsa

1 small red onion, peeled and finely chopped
2 teaspoons capers, washed
1 cup fresh walnuts, coarsely chopped
2 tablespoons sherry wine vinegar
¼ cup olive oil
sea salt and freshly ground black pepper to taste

Place all the ingredients in a blender or food processor and pulse until combined.

MAKES ABOUT 1 ½ CUPS

117

Cinnamon and Sumac Chicken

Soak the wooden skewers for 1 hour in water before threading the meat onto them.

6 boneless chicken thighs
1 tablespoon extra virgin olive oil
1½ teaspoons sumac
1½ teaspoons ground cinnamon
1 tablespoon grated orange zest
2 tablespoons orange juice
1 tablespoon runny honey

Cut the chicken thighs in half lengthways and thread onto the skewers. Combine the rest of the ingredients in a bowl and mix together. Place the chicken skewers in a shallow dish and pour over the marinade (use a brush to apply extra mixture over the chicken). Cover and refrigerate for 1 hour prior to cooking, brushing the chicken occasionally.

Grill the chicken on a barbecue plate over medium to high heat for 3–4 minutes each side, brushing with any remaining marinade as they cook.

SERVES 6

Turtle Bean and Avocado Salad

200g turtle beans, rinsed and drained
1 teaspoon salt
2 firm ripe avocados, peeled, stoned and diced
3 firm ripe tomatoes, peeled, deseeded and chopped
¼ cup chopped chives

DRESSING
3 tablespoons verjuice
3 tablespoons olive oil
2 tablespoons sherry vinegar
1 tablespoon lemon juice
sea salt and freshly ground black pepper to taste

Cook the turtle beans in plenty of water with the salt until tender. Rinse beans under cold water, drain and mop up any excess water from them with absorbent kitchen paper.

Place the beans, avocado, tomato and chives in a serving bowl. Whisk together the dressing ingredients, then drizzle over the salad and gently combine. Cover and allow to stand at room temperature for 30 minutes before serving to allow the flavours to merge.

SERVES 6–8

Cinnamon and sumac chicken
with turtle bean and avocado salad

Barbecued Pearl Perch

While freshly caught pearl perch are a delicious treat, this recipe will work just as well with any other fleshy fish with a snapper-like texture.

4 x 200g whole pearl perch, cleaned and scaled
freshly ground black pepper and flaky sea salt
¼ cup extra virgin olive oil
¼ cup lemon juice
1 red onion, peeled, halved and thinly sliced
2 firm ripe tomatoes, skinned, deseeded and thinly sliced
1 red pepper (capsicum), skinned, deseeded and thinly sliced
handful of fresh coriander leaves
shredded zest of 1 lemon
red wine vinegar
olive oil
lemon wedges for garnishing

Preheat the barbecue grill. Make a couple of deep slashes in the thickest part of each fish, then pat dry with absorbent kitchen paper inside and out. Season well and drizzle with the olive oil and lemon juice.

Barbecue the fish on the hot grill for 4–5 minutes each side or until the flesh of the fish flakes when tested with a knife.

Combine the onion, tomato, pepper, coriander and lemon zest. Drizzle some red vinegar and olive oil over the salad to moisten. Serve the fish straight from the barbecue with the salad on the side.

SERVES 4

Honey Soy Butterflied Char-roasted Chicken

2 corn-fed chickens
3 cloves garlic, peeled and grated
4 tablespoons runny honey
3 tablespoons Dijon mustard
2 tablespoons dark soy sauce
1 tablespoon dry sherry
1 tablespoon lemon juice
olive oil

Pat dry the chickens with absorbent kitchen paper. Using a pair of kitchen scissors, cut along each side of the backbone. Lift out and discard (backbones can be frozen and used for chicken stock). Turn the chickens skin-side up and press down to flatten them.

Combine the garlic, honey, mustard, soy sauce, sherry and lemon juice. Using a sharp knife, make deep slash marks through the skin of the drumsticks and thighs. Massage the marinade well into the surface area of both chickens. Cover and refrigerate for 1 hour.

Preheat the oven to 180°C. Place the chickens in a roasting pan and roast for 30 minutes. Remove the chickens from the oven and finish cooking them, covered, over medium heat on a barbecue grill for a further 20–30 minutes, basting them from time to time with the remaining marinade and a little olive oil until they are cooked through. Place the chickens on a serving platter and spoon over the remaining marinade and juices.

SERVES 8–10

Potato Smash

A great way to revive leftover new potatoes – either in the oven or on the barbecue plate. You can also prepare them from scratch, in which case it's best to parboil them first.

16 small round new potatoes
2 tablespoons olive oil
sea salt and freshly ground black pepper
fresh rosemary leaves

Preheat the oven to 250°C or the barbecue to a high heat. Place the potatoes on a baking tray or on the barbecue hot plate. Use a potato masher to squash each potato flat. Drizzle over the olive oil and season generously. Sprinkle the rosemary leaves over the squashed potato. Cook for 20 minutes or until crisp and golden, turning halfway through cooking whichever method is used.

SERVES 4–6

Honey soy butterflied char-roasted chicken

Marinated Barbecued Lamb Shoulder

1.5kg boned lamb shoulder
2 cloves garlic, peeled and grated
¼ cup extra virgin olive oil
¼ cup chopped fresh mint
2 tablespoons verjuice
2 tablespoons sea salt

LEMON AND MINT SAUCE
½ cup extra virgin olive oil
¼ cup verjuice
3 tablespoons chopped chives
3 tablespoons chopped fresh mint
chopped rind of 3 preserved lemons, flesh discarded
1 tablespoon lemon juice

Pierce the meat all over with a wooden skewer or a sharply pointed long thin knife. Combine the garlic, olive oil, mint, verjuice and salt. Smother the meat with the marinade, rubbing it in until it is all absorbed. Refrigerate for several hours or overnight.

Preheat the barbecue to high heat. Sear the meat all over until the skin is well browned. Remove from the barbecue plate and wrap the lamb in aluminium foil so it is well sealed. Place it back on the barbecue and cook for 30 minutes over medium heat or until the meat is medium–rare. Remove the foil for the last 5 minutes of cooking.

Combine the sauce ingredients. Remove the lamb from the barbecue and place in a shallow dish. Pour over the sauce and allow it to rest for 15–20 minutes before carving.

SERVES 6

Marinated barbecued lamb shoulder

Prosciutto-wrapped Lamb Cutlets

16 French lamb cutlets
2 tablespoons Dijon mustard
16 thin slices prosciutto
16 sprigs rosemary

Lay the cutlets flat on a chopping board and spread with a little mustard. Wrap each cutlet in a slice of prosciutto and insert a sprig of rosemary. Grill the cutlets on a hot barbecue grill for approximately 3 minutes on each side or until the prosciutto is crisp and the lamb medium–rare.

SERVES 4

Feta and Chickpea Salad

300g canned chickpeas, washed and drained
150g cow's feta cheese, crumbled
1 Lebanese cucumber, peeled, deseeded
  and diced
4 spring onions, sliced
¼ cup chopped flat-leafed parsley
¼ cup chopped coriander leaves
1 cup cherry tomatoes, halved
¼ cup extra virgin olive oil
2 tablespoons lemon juice
sea salt and freshly ground black pepper to taste

Place the chickpeas in a saucepan and cover with plenty of cold salted water. Simmer until tender, then drain and rinse under cold water. Remove any excess water from the chickpeas with absorbent kitchen paper. Place the chickpeas, feta, cucumber, spring onions, herbs and tomatoes in a serving bowl. Drizzle over the olive oil and lemon juice and season to taste. Gently toss salad together and allow to sit for 1 hour at room temperature before serving.

SERVES 6–8

Glazed Barbecued Pork Chops

8 pork loin chops
¼ cup soy sauce
4 tablespoons tomato sauce
4 tablespoons hoisin sauce
2 tablespoons balsamic vinegar
2 tablespoons dry sherry
¼ cup brown sugar

Using a sharp knife, cut slashes at 4cm intervals through the skin and fat of each chop. Place the remaining ingredients in a food processor and pulse together. Place the chops in a shallow dish and pour over the marinade. Cover and refrigerate for 1 hour.

Grill the meat on a medium to hot barbecue plate for 8–10 minutes on each side, basting from time to time as it cooks.

SERVES 8

Prosciutto-wrapped lamb cutlets
with feta and chickpea salad

Grilled rump and vegetables with char-roasted
balsamic and rosemary onions

Grilled Rump and Vegetables

Succulent and full of flavour, barbecued rump and grilled summer vegetables are combined here in a hearty one-platter meal. Alternatively, pile it all into split French sticks for a hand-held sandwich.

3 tablespoons olive oil
3 cloves garlic, peeled and grated
2 teaspoons ground cumin
1 teaspoon ground coriander
2 tablespoons lemon juice
2 x 600g pieces rump steak, 5cm thick
2 red peppers (capsicums)
2 yellow peppers (capsicums)
18 asparagus spears
1 red onion, peeled and thickly sliced
olive oil for cooking
sea salt
fresh coriander sprigs

Combine the olive oil, garlic, cumin, coriander and lemon juice in a shallow dish. Coat the meat with the marinade, cover and refrigerate overnight.

Cut the peppers into four lengthways. Remove the core and seeds, then cut each quarter in half, again lengthways. Snap the hard ends from the asparagus. Brush the vegetables with olive oil and season with a little sea salt. Grill the beef and vegetables over medium to high heat until the vegetables are lightly charred and tender and the steak medium–rare. Keep the vegetables warm and allow the meat to rest for 5 minutes. Cut the meat into 1cm slices and layer it on a platter with the grilled vegetables. Garnish with the coriander sprigs and serve with crusty bread to mop up the juices.

SERVES 6–8

Char-roasted Balsamic and Rosemary Onions

These sweet caramelised onions and fragrant rosemary sprigs marry well with roasted and barbecued red meats.

6 medium onions (a mix of brown, white and red)
3 tablespoons balsamic vinegar
3 tablespoons olive oil
1 tablespoon chopped fresh rosemary
sea salt and freshly ground black pepper
fresh rosemary sprigs and leaves for garnishing
2 tablespoons peppery extra virgin olive oil

Preheat the oven to 180°C. Peel and cut the onions in half through the middle. Arrange the onions cut-side down in a roasting pan and sprinkle with the vinegar, olive oil and rosemary. Roast for 25–30 minutes. Finish off the cooking on a medium-hot barbecue grill for about 5 minutes on each side. Arrange in a serving dish and sprinkle over the seasonings, remaining fresh rosemary and extra virgin olive oil.

SERVES 4–6

Spiced Barbecue Chicken with Mango and Yoghurt Sauce

¾ cup store-bought tandoori paste
1 cup plain acidophilus yoghurt
2 tablespoons lime juice
8 skinless and boneless chicken thighs
lime wedges for garnishing

Combine the tandoori paste, yoghurt and lime juice in a bowl. Cut the chicken thighs into thick strips and toss them in the tandoori mixture until well coated. Cover with plastic food wrap and refrigerate for 1 hour.

Barbecue the chicken strips over a medium–hot preheated grill for 8–10 minutes, turning once, until cooked through. Pile the strips onto a platter and serve with the Mango and Yoghurt Sauce (see below) and lime wedges.

Mango and Yoghurt Sauce

1 mango, skinned and flesh chopped
2 tablespoons fresh coriander leaves
1 tablespoon fresh mint leaves
sea salt and white pepper to taste
1½ cups plain acidophilus yoghurt
½ telegraph cucumber, peeled, deseeded and coarsely grated

Place the mango, herbs, seasonings and yoghurt in a food processor and pulse until smooth. Spoon into a bowl. Drain the grated cucumber on absorbent kitchen paper for 5 minutes, then stir it through the yoghurt mixture. Cover and refrigerate for 1 hour before serving with the chicken.

SERVES 4

Grape Brûlée

2 cups seedless red grapes
500g mascarpone
1 teaspoon vanilla extract
caster sugar

Place the grapes in an ovenproof baking dish just large enough to take a single layer of grapes. Combine the mascarpone and vanilla extract and spread it evenly over the top of the grapes. Sprinkle an even layer of caster sugar over the top of the mascarpone. Place the dish under a medium–hot grill for approximately 8–10 minutes to melt and caramelise the sugar. Remove from the grill and allow to cool. Once cool, transfer the brulée to the refrigerator to chill and set before serving.

SERVES 6

Tropical Fruit Salad with Rum Syrup

½ rock melon, skinned, deseeded and diced
½ cantaloupe melon, skinned, deseeded and diced
1 mango, skinned and flesh diced
1 ripe pineapple, skinned, cored and diced
1 cup dark rum
2 kaffir lime leaves, shredded
1 tablespoon sugar
4 passionfruit, halved and pulp reserved

Place the diced fruit in a bowl. In a saucepan heat the rum, kaffir lime leaves, sugar and passionfruit pulp until the sugar is dissolved. Cool the syrup and pour it over the fruit. Place in the refrigerator for 1 hour before serving. Serve in chilled glasses.

SERVES 8

Grape brûlée

Sponge Fingers

*These look and taste wonderful served with some summer berries,
such as redcurrants, strawberries, raspberries or boysenberries,
on the side.*

**16 store-bought Italian sponge fingers,
halved lengthways**

CREAM CUSTARD FILLING
300ml thickened cream
1 cup milk
½ cup caster sugar
1 teaspoon vanilla extract
4 egg yolks
2 tablespoons cornflour
2 tablespoons butter

icing sugar for garnishing

Combine the cream, milk, sugar and vanilla in a saucepan and bring to the boil,
then remove from heat. In a bowl beat together the egg yolks and cornflour
until thick and creamy. Gradually beat in the hot cream mixture and return the
custard to the heat, stirring with a whisk until it boils and thickens. Remove
from the heat and stir in the butter. Cover with plastic food wrap and allow to
cool thoroughly.

About 1 hour before serving, spread half of the sponge fingers with the
custard and sandwich with the remaining sponge fingers. Cover and allow to
stand at room temperature. Just before serving, dust the tops with icing sugar
and serve 2 per person.

SERVES 8

Sponge fingers

glossary

Blind bake
This involves partially baking a pie shell or similar that has dried beans or rice in it to weigh it down so the pastry can't rise.

Bocconcini
Small fresh balls of mozzarella cheese, the New Zealand version is usually made from cow's milk, but the best is made from buffalo's milk. However, as they are imported from Italy, they can be an expensive and highly perishable treat.

Dutch cocoa
A superior cocoa powder available at specialty food shops, it differs from standard cocoa in that it has been treated with an alkali that neutralises the cocoa's natural acidity.

Dukkah
This combination of coarsely ground nuts, seeds and spices (sometimes spelt as dukka) is popular as a snack and for coating different food items. It's usually made up of toasted hazelnuts, toasted sesame seeds, coriander seeds and sometimes mustard seeds, sea salt, coarsely ground black pepper and oil. You can make it up yourself or buy it ready-made from most supermarkets.

Haloumi cheese
Absolutely delicious grilled or fried, haloumi cheese originated in Cyprus and is readily available in delicatessens and specialty food shops. Haloumi is traditionally made from goat's milk, but in New Zealand it's also made from cow's or sheep's milk – and sometimes a blend of both.

Kecap manis
Sweetened with palm sugar and seasoned with various ingredients including garlic and star anise, this dark brown, syrupy Indonesian sauce is used as flavouring in various Indonesian dishes and as a condiment. It keeps well and is available from Asian food shops.

Lime 'cheeks'
Lime cheeks are simply limes that have been cut in half through the middle. I like to call them cheeks because that's what their plump shape reminds me of.

Limoncello
This is an intensely sweet lemony Italian liqueur that traditionally comes from Sicily, but there is also a New Zealand version available.

Mascarpone
Italian in origin, this is a rich, soft ivory-coloured double cream made from cow's milk and which is freely available. Perfect to serve alongside desserts, especially cakes and puddings.

Palm sugar
A dark coarse unrefined sugar, usually sold in solid cake form so it's easy to grate as little or as much as required. Palm sugar often features in Asian-style cooking and is available at most supermarkets.

Passata
Another traditional Italian ingredient, passata is simply sauce made from passing fresh tomatoes through a sieve. Now, of course, you don't have to do it yourself because it's available from most delicatessens and specialty food shops.

Pomelo
This giant citrus fruit (also known as shaddock, after an English sea captain) is native to Malaysia and has a very thick, soft rind that can vary in colour from yellow to pale yellowish-brown to pink.

Porcini powder
Made from porcini mushrooms, an Italian speciality, this intensely flavoured and highly aromatic powder can be used in sauces as well as in pasta and risotto dishes and is available from most delicatessens and specialty food shops.

Prosciutto
This delicious seasoned Italian ham gets its flavour and texture by being

salt cured and air dried. Prosciutto is available at delicatessens and specialty food shops.

Sambal oelek
A mix of chillies, brown sugar and salt usually served as an accompaniment to rice and curry dishes and easily available. Variations can include candlenuts, garlic, kaffir lime leaves, onion, galangal, tamarind concentrate and sometimes coconut milk.

Sumac
Usually available in ground form, sumac is a popular Middle Eastern spice, dark red in colour and available from supermarkets. It's used to add a touch of tartness to a variety of savoury dishes.

Tamarind water
To make tamarind water, simply soak some tamarind pulp concentrate in the required amount of water. The fruit of a tall shade tree native to Asia and northern Africa and widely grown in India, tamarind comes in various forms: concentrated pulp with seeds, canned paste, whole pods dried into 'bricks' or ground into powder – all available from Asian food shops.

Turtle beans
These dried beans with their black skin, cream-coloured flesh and sweet flavour are also known as black beans and have long been popular in Mexico, Central and South America, the Caribbean and the southern United States. They are commonly available.

Verjuice
The juice of unripe grapes crushed and strained, verjuice (also known as verjus) is usually made from grapes that are high in acid and low in sugar. It's often used in vinaigrettes and sauces and with fish and poultry, and it is excellent for deglazing pans.

Zatar
Also spelt as zahtar and zaatar, this is a combination of ground sumac, sesame seeds and dried thyme available from delicatessens and specialty food shops. Use it mixed with oil as a spread for bread or sprinkle it over meat and vegetables.

NZ/AUSTRALIA	US	GREAT BRITAIN
Beetroot	beet	beetroot
Pepper (capsicum)	bell pepper	pepper
Caster sugar	superfine sugar	caster sugar
Coriander	cilantro	coriander
Cornflour	cornstarch	cornflour
Cream	whipping cream	whipping cream
Eggplant	eggplant	aubergine
Grill	broil	grill
Icing sugar	confectioner's sugar	icing sugar
Ground beef	ground beef	minced beef
Plain flour	all-purpose flour	plain flour
Prawn	shrimp	prawn
Self-raising flour	self-rising flour	self-raising flour
Sultanas	seedless white raisins	sultanas
Tasty cheese	cheddar or jack cheese	cheddar cheese
Tomato purée	tomato paste	tomato purée
Zucchini	zucchini	courgette

weights & measures

Abbreviations

g	gram
kg	kilogram
mm	millimetre
cm	centimetre
ml	millilitre
°C	degrees Celsius

Weight conversions

NZ METRIC	IMPERIAL/US
25g	1 oz
50g	2 oz
75g	3 oz
100g	3½ oz
125g	4½ oz
150g	5 oz
175g	6 oz
200g	7 oz
225g	8 oz
250g	9 oz
275g	9½ oz
300g	10½ oz
325g	11½ oz
350g	12½ oz
375g	13 oz
400g	14 oz
450g	16 oz (1 lb)
500g	17½ oz
750g	26½ oz
1kg	35 oz (2¼ lb)

Length conversions

METRIC	IMPERIAL/US
0.5cm (5mm)	¼ inch
1cm	½ inch
2.5cm	1 inch
5cm	2 inches
10cm	4 inches
20cm	8 inches
30cm	12 inches (1 foot)

Liquid conversions

NZ METRIC	IMPERIAL	US
5ml (1 teaspoon)	¼ fl oz	1 teaspoon
15ml (1 tablespoon)	½ fl oz	1 tablespoon
30ml (⅛ cup)	1 fl oz	⅛ cup
60ml (¼ cup)	2 fl oz	¼ cup
125ml (½ cup)	4 fl oz	½ cup
150ml	5 fl oz (¼ pint)	⅔ cup
175ml	6 fl oz	¾ cup
250ml (1 cup)	8 fl oz	1 cup (½ pint)
300ml	10 fl oz (½ pint)	1¼ cups
375ml	12 fl oz	1½ cups
500ml (2 cups)	16 fl oz	2 cups (1 pint)
600ml	20 fl oz (1 pint)	2½ cups

NB The Australian metric tablespoon measures 20ml

Temperature conversions

CELSIUS	FAHRENHEIT	GAS
100°C	225°F	¼
125°C	250°F	½
150°C	300°F	2
160°C	325°F	3
170°C	325°F	3
180°C	350°F	4
190°C	375°F	5
200°C	400°F	6
210°C	425°F	7
220°C	425°F	7
230°C	450°F	8
250°C	500°F	9

Cake tin sizes

METRIC	IMPERIAL/US
15cm	6 inches
18cm	7 inches
20cm	8 inches
23cm	9 inches
25cm	10 inches
28cm	11 inches

index

acknowledgements

Lifestyle cookbooks require special collaboration, and I would like to thank the very talented people who helped create this stunning sequel to *Beach Bach Boat Barbecue*. Thank you so much to the team at New Holland, who as always make it all look easy. Thank you also to editor Renée Lang for her guidance, wealth of experience and damn good company. Ian Batchelor has yet again captured the essence of our New Zealand land- and seascapes and summer lifestyle with his insightful images and truly edible food photography. All this has been beautifully put together by Christine Hansen, who has recreated a fresh and updated design with her usual flare. Thank you also to Kate and Barry Hastings of Waiheke Island who graciously lent their paradise as a backdrop to many a shot. My thanks also to Julie Fay from Palm Beach, and to Rose Gresson of Telegraph Hill for all their olives and olive oils. I hope you all enjoy the food and ambiance of our happy collaboration.

Penny Oliver

Without the enduring help of many, projects such as this would not see the light of day. My thanks go to Belinda Cooke and the rest of the team at New Holland who have encouraged and cajoled in equal measure; to Penny, who is always fun to work with and provides great food for me to eat after I've photographed it; to Christine Hansen for the delicate way she combines the food photography with the environmental photographs, breathing life into the book; and to all those who have helped by providing locations that have inspired the photographs. These include Te Mahia Bay Resort, Golden Bay Vineyard, NZ Junket and many friends and family who have put up with me and my camera.

Ian Batchelor

p 25, 28, 40, 49, 50, 52, 54, 60, 63, 64, 76, 79
82, 91, 95, 103, 108, 122, 124, 126, 134